Avoidance Doesn't Work

# Avoidance Doesn't Work

## - making life better -

### Iain Scott

*This book is dedicated to my friend
and colleague Jonathan Brauner.*

*Margaret Thatcher once said
"Everyone should have a Willie"
- failing to understand why the gathered
journalists found this so funny
and referring to Willie Whitelaw
(then Home Secretary).
From my experience, I would say that
"Everyone should have a Jonathan."*

First published in 2012 by HPT Books

HPT Books is part of
The Human Potential Trust
The Oasis
Highbrook Lane
West Hoathly
Sussex  RH19 4PL
England

A catalogue record for this book is available from the British Library.

Proceeds from the sale of this book,
including the author's/photographer's royalties,
will be used for our charitable work.

ISBN 978-1-899131-06-8

Printed and bound by Tien Wah Press (Pte) Ltd, Singapore

**Title page:** *We named this zebra foal "Avoidance Doesn't Work"
to stress the importance of what needs to be understood.*

# Contents

# Introduction

One possible title for this book was "Seven billion people can be wrong." It was seriously suggested a number of months ago by my friend and colleague, Jonathan, to whom this book is dedicated. We rejected it, mainly because such a title might suggest arrogance on my part - and I'm certainly not arrogant - yet here I am starting off the introduction to this book by mentioning it.

My neighbour, Peter, is 80 years of age and has reached the conclusion during his long lifetime that the human race is "flawed". He has seen the same fundamental mistakes made over and over again, including war after war, as if people were incapable of learning or being logical. He has seen politicians repeatedly fail to live up to their promises. He is dismayed by a severe lack of common sense, whereas lazy-mindedness combined with bluff is everywhere.

Edgar D. Mitchell was the sixth man to walk on the moon. Like the other astronauts and cosmonauts, he returned from space profoundly affected by the experience of seeing our home planet from a distance - certain that the human race needed a similar shift in perspective. Later, he was completely convinced that my brain functions in a very different way to that of other human beings. Ed Mitchell kindly endorsed my first book, *Human Potential - the search for that "something more"*, with his words appearing on the back cover. What I have never publicly

***Right and far right:***
*If humans had as much curiosity and alertness as wild animals such as this coyote and yellow-footed rock-wallaby, learning might happen more readily.*

> *"I am completely convinced that Iain Scott's rare experience is likely a part of the evolutionary destiny of Homo sapiens."*
>
> Edgar D. Mitchell

said or written about until now is that he didn't think people would be sufficiently interested to actually learn how to do what I had achieved - despite their claimed intent. Instead of explaining the "how to" stuff, Ed Mitchell suggested I should write about myself - what he called "the adventures of a hero".

But this has never been about me and that first book went ahead, published exactly as planned, with just a few introductory pages at the beginning to explain what had happened to me. The book sold well and I received many letters from readers expressing further interest. I know that some have read and re-read it many dozens of times and others hundreds of times. It has been described as "like Shakespeare", with level after level of meaning. I did my best to make sure it was very simply written. Yet I am almost certain that nobody has fully understood everything, or at least fully applied everything.

My next book was called *Actions Speak Louder Than Words*, suggesting the need for a no-nonsense approach. I didn't say anything further about myself, other than briefly repeating a bit from the previous book - again, as a necessary explanation as to why I was writing about the subject of an improved psychology or better way of being. The text was intentionally hard-hitting, described by some as "not ideal reading material for bedtime". Not surprisingly, I received fewer letters than before.

The next three books focused on nature conservation and the environment. I'll come back to this subject shortly (and later on), but I'm briefly mentioning it now to make the point that I didn't need to explain much about myself in these more recent publications.

Now, 18 years on, I consider it is appropriate to write a bit more about my "adventures" as Ed Mitchell earlier advised. That said, this is far from being anything like an autobiography. It is not a book about myself nor my life, in any conventional sense. As before, I am writing for you and about you.

I appreciate that I have said very little so far, but nevertheless hope the above is enough of an introduction to stimulate your curiosity so that you will read further. Before finishing, I should add a few quick words about the overall presentation of this book. Rather than just producing a text-only publication, we decided to add a number of

my photographic images. These illustrate and hopefully emphasise our deliberate "actions speak louder than words" policy, many of the images capturing aspects of our own practical work in the areas of nature conservation and humanitarian aid. This will become clearer as you read on.....

*Above:  A field of wild poppies - the symbol for remembrance.  My neighbour has seen war after war during his long lifetime.*

Iain Scott
Sussex, March 2012

# 1

# Undeniable

## i. Breakthrough

The first question I asked myself was "Am I going mad?" The answer was obvious - no, in case you're wondering - because what I had just experienced embraced more understanding, logic, and clarity than anything I had previously known. And it offered undeniable benefits, to put it mildly. But I had to check by asking such questions. Although only 18 years old, I was already evidence-based in my thinking, convinced through education by the scientific method of how to work out fact from fiction. Everything can be explained, but assumptions can be dangerous pitfalls. I knew that what had just happened to me was too important to get wrong. I made myself a promise, right then at the beginning, to figure out precisely what was going on. And I did.

It started late one evening way back in the summer of 1975, when I suddenly experienced an astonishing expansion of consciousness. Timeless moments of ecstasy, oneness, and understanding revealed a reality I had not previously considered. There was an intense awareness of the unity of everything and everyone. Life had an obvious meaning and purpose. This mental awareness was matched by an

*Right and far right:* "It is
*better to have lived as a tiger*
*for a single day, than as a*
*sheep for a thousand years."*
*(Tibetan proverb)*

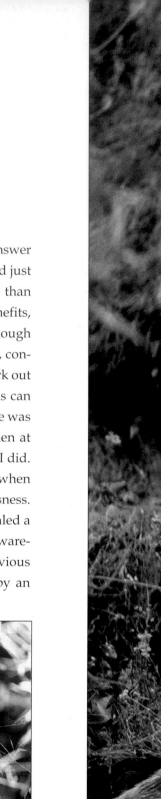

12

*Above: I lived in the Lake District during my early childhood.*

equally intense feeling of love, caring, and belonging. I could clearly see the problems facing our world and also a solution to them. This was accompanied by an incredible sense of needing to help others - not in any compulsive or unbalanced way, but simply because service was the indisputable thing to do. Any selfish tendencies had dropped away, although I still retained an appreciation of individuality. There was no sense of separateness, only oneness.

I'm going to briefly pause at this point to hopefully reassure you that I'm not some nutter or religious maniac. I am not in the slightest bit delusional, nor remotely interested in self-promotion. The leading academics who have affirmed my authenticity are not idiots or easily fooled. And, besides, my mother-in-law once said that I'm "normal". If it made best sense to do so, I would have written this book with no mention of myself. But, to repeat, Ed Mitchell's advice had some merit. So I'll continue.....

Dozens of additional oneness experiences followed in the days and weeks ahead, each of them consolidating what had initially occurred through a process of purification and transformation. I never tried to initiate them; they seemingly just happened spontaneously. I told a friend what was happening to me, using the description of feeling smaller than the smallest ant yet bigger than the biggest mountain. As a child, I lived in the Lake District and later studied colonies of ants - thus the terminology for this inadequate expression.

During this early stage, I can remember one particular incident that makes a relevant point. In the physical time that it took me to leave my room, walk to the bathroom next door, use the toilet, wash my hands, then return to my room, I underwent not one but three distinct inner transformations or oneness experiences. Each involved a series of timeless moments and considerable understanding. Yet this had all occurred in a matter of a few minutes, clearly indicating an accelerated mental process. (I wasn't constipated, nor slow thinking, before any of this began.)

I moved to London in late September to continue my education. Various interactions with other people quickly confirmed that I had changed more than I had perhaps realised. For example, I was already unusually open in comparison to those around me. Meanwhile, the oneness experiences continued.

True to my promise, I had managed to work out quite a lot by now. I understood that I was slipping in and out of two distinctly different mindsets. The normal "me, first" or self-orientated mindset had progressively weakened and now appeared to be grossly limited or even stupid. But habit nevertheless pulled me back into this normalised selfish mentality every time a oneness experience faded, despite the powerful afterglow and transformative effects. It was as if I had been pre-programmed to respond in a self-orientated way - which, of course, was true. Everyone is massively influenced by social conditioning. Monkey do what monkey see.

Back then, it was like having two clashing maps or blueprints in my mind. Thankfully, any internal conflict was minimal - as it was almost always blatantly obvious which was best. I had understood and accepted that I was a stranger in a strange land. I recognised the compelling conceptual integrity and practical benefits of my "new" blueprint for life, even if some of the attachments of the old habitual

*"Let go, it's over."*

Eminem

*"Without prior reading in the area, you nevertheless achieved states which mirror exactly those recorded by mystics in all the great spiritual traditions. This provides further proof of the authenticity of your experience."*

Professor David Fontana

*Above: As a teenager, I bred butterflies and moths. This process of transformation was like a caterpillar repeatedly shedding its skin as it grew and developed.*

patterns remained. But sometimes I would nonetheless find myself still being selfish. For example, in a conversation, I might sometimes say something that the "new" and by now biggest part of me didn't mean or even agree with. Rapidly, within a second or two, I was able to cut myself short in mid-sentence. I would apologise for being selfish and re-start from my true or better perspective. These were very minor blips but clear indications that the transformation process was still incomplete.

I realised that everyone I ever met was stuck with just the one basic mindset. Each person experienced conflict and dilemma with regards to conscience or differing aspirations, of course, but they were overall dominated by the normalised self-orientated way of living life. They didn't have a choice, as I had. Later on, when I came across individuals who had experienced a oneness experience or two themselves, any benefits were nevertheless negligible with the usual "me, me, me" mentality still firmly in control.

So I learnt a lot about the differences between these two mindsets by observing the behaviour of others, understanding what caused or limited this behaviour. It all provided a glaring contrast to the alternative I now knew and mostly responded to. And the occasional blips in myself confirmed these same patterns. It was like knowing two different languages, only much more so.

This "new" consciousness was a complete surprise to me. When it began, I hadn't heard of anyone else having oneness experiences, nor had I read any book on the subject. I wasn't religious and I certainly didn't meditate. And - in case you're wondering - I hadn't taken LSD, magic mushrooms, or any other mind-expanding drug. I had no prior knowledge whatsoever of what happened.

In London, I eventually came across various books on spiritual development and mysticism. On the whole, I found them lacking in the extreme. Yes, some confirmed that such experiences were known and had occurred to others. But precise and practical knowledge was shockingly limited. It seemed to me that the subject was poorly understood and that I already knew much more. A short book called *Jonathan Livingston Seagull* by Richard Bach was at least reassuring, if still somewhat vague in detail.

Eventually, in 1978, a final realisation or insight removed the last mental barrier or habitual link to the old, ordinary consciousness. The transformation process was complete. I laughed at how slow I had been to see through the final illusion of self. To me, the enlightenment was staggering, although a close friend commented that it was more like the final dotting of i's and crossing of t's. Looking back, we were both right.

## ii.  First attempts

*"He who knows*
*does not speak.*
*He who speaks*
*does not know."*

Lao Tsu

People are far too quick to believe a load of nonsense - a topic I'll come back to later on. One of the questionable "spiritual truisms" that has done the rounds over many years is "Those who genuinely know, do not speak." Lao Tsu, a 6th century Chinese philosopher, probably started this off.

It would be contradictory to expect someone who knows not to speak, as this would go against service before self. Others would be deprived of the possibility of learning. That said, this subject matter is the ultimate example of that which is ineffable. Misunderstandings are to be expected, to some degree, especially early on.

Anyway, I started to speak out - at first answering questions from those who already knew me. We were quickly joined by others they knew, and so on. Before long, I was regularly meeting with between two and three hundred people each week, usually in small groups but sometimes on a one-to-one basis. In those days, not long after the "peace, love, and understanding" of the late '60s and early '70s, quite a few people were interested in changing themselves.

*Far right:*
*Can you "think big"?*

Almost everyone said they were being helped. But I was sceptical. Yes, they were thinking about things more - and this thinking was even a bit more precise. And, yes, they were feeling more. However, something was missing. They were only "changing" internally, with

*Above:* A hedgehog and bluebells at The Oasis nature reserve.

little outward expression or evidence of this claimed "progress". From my perspective, it became increasingly clear that this was just pseudo-change and not the real thing.

I did my best to explain what was missing, but the encouragement seemed to fall on deaf ears. The situation wasn't helped by the popular belief that spiritual or personal development is an internal thing. Meat Loaf's blockbuster album *Bat Out of Hell* had not long been released and I jokingly told everyone that another of his well-known songs - *Two Out of Three Ain't Bad* - didn't apply here. It was crucial to think more, care more, AND do more. The penny still didn't drop.

I was aware that all the previous attempts to communicate this different way of being by oddities similar to myself had ultimately failed. It was obvious. Everyone was still stuck in the self-orientated mindset and any knowledge or guidance on how to break out of it seemed limited and muddled. Now my first attempts were failing too. Those around me, however, strongly disagreed; they were sure that they were changing.

Knowing I was right, I decided to re-think my whole strategy. After giving everyone two weeks' notice so they could ask any outstanding questions, I moved on. There were protests, of course, from several groups who tried to convince me that they and I were indeed "on track". But this clarity of mind allows no room for self-deception, so that was that.

## iii. Plugging the gap

A more action-based approach was clearly needed. In 1981, I bought 9 acres of land in Sussex and started The Oasis - a nature reserve and education centre. The idea was to combine an interest in searching for that "something more" with practical nature conservation work. I was still prepared to answer questions, but only if someone was willing to simultaneously get their hands dirty. Our "actions speak louder than words" policy was underway.

With the help of a friend, I set up a British registered charity called The Wildlife For All Trust to facilitate this nature conservation work. We purposely decided to work on a non-paid basis; (I have financially supported myself by growing plants). We have always specialised in "forgotten" species or habitats that other organisations have ignored. In the early years, our main focus was endangered Australian wallabies. Two wallaby species, all captive bred, were kept at The Oasis in large enclosures for educational purposes. We also worked in Australia, encouraging the relevant government authorities and farmers to do more. We then expanded our projects, beginning in 1992, by working to save the critically endangered geometric tortoise in South Africa, as well as contributing to the survival of the rare natterjack toad here in the UK.

As I am rapidly whizzing through the years, I should also throw in at this point that we worked in Ethiopia and Sudan for 25 years carrying out humanitarian aid. It began during the 1984/1985 famine, after which our initial relief work in Ethiopia then became a long-term development project in Sudan - with a medical clinic at the heart of this enterprise. Again, we did this work non-paid.

*"Part of the world that you live in. You are the part that you're giving."*

*Carpet of the Sun*
Renaissance

*Above:  Komsberg is a big place.*

*Right:  We have a good population of meerkats at Komsberg.*

Returning to our wildlife work, in 2002 we purchased 16,000 acres in South Africa and established Komsberg Wilderness Nature Reserve. This was effectively doubled in size in 2006 when we then bought a neighbouring sheep farm, thus making Komsberg over 30,000 acres or 125 sq km in size. It is a very big place. We had previously started The Tortoise Farm nature reserve, also in South Africa, to further our efforts to save the geometric tortoise from extinction.

Meanwhile, we set up The Human Potential Trust (another British registered charity) with the aim of providing reliable knowledge and education about how to overcome the self-orientated mindset. This understanding, of course, has underpinned our many achievements in the fields of nature conservation and humanitarian aid. It has greatly increased our project effectiveness and efficiency - making us different from other organisations. The key to our success is attitude.

# 2
# Basics

## i. Education

*"Our schools are not teaching students to think.
It is astonishing how many young people have difficulty in putting
their brains definitely and systematically to work."*

Thomas Edison

I have always maintained that what has happened to me is simply an evolutionary step forward. This potential is theoretically available to anyone with a normally functioning brain. It is not a matter of having different genetics and it has nothing whatsoever to do with belief. The way forward is determined by education. However, there needs to be an improved and coherent form of education - one that is evidence-based and far-reaching. We need to learn to "think big", realistically and precisely, incorporating all of the important issues from personal to global. Nothing must be avoided.

Education comes mainly from family upbringing, school, the peer pressure of others, and the media. Parental behaviour provides most of the crucial early influences and there is a lot of truth in the saying

**Right:** *Burchell's zebra are re-introduced to Komsberg after an absence of 197 years.*

**Far right:** *The first foal is born.*

*Above:  Education is critically important.*

"Show me the five-year-old boy and I'll show you the man." School should, of course, provide a fair opportunity for all - correcting and compensating for any early imbalances if necessary. But it usually doesn't. The school system appears to be more geared up to sorting out the clever from the not-so-clever (that's when it's not trying to massage exam results to give an overestimation of what is considered to be clever). Meanwhile, the pupils learn which group they fit into: the popular or the unpopular, the have's or the have-not's, the bullies or the bullied, the sporty or the not-so-sporty, and so on. Going on to do further education doesn't seem to achieve much more.

Being a gregarious species, humans generally feel the need to fit in and be accepted. So the influence of others throughout adulthood is likely to result in just more of the same. And the media usually feeds us what most people want. As much of it is commercially driven, paid for by advertising, the term "mass media" appears justified because popular appeal means a bigger audience.

It's therefore hardly surprising that surveys have shown more than half of British schoolgirls aged 13 to 19 nowadays aspire to become a footballer's wife or girlfriend - as an easy route to having lots of money. Many likewise dream of becoming the next pop star to shoot to instant fame and fortune on a television talent show, especially when talent often seems less important than image. In fact, nearly two out of three young women want to be famous. Meanwhile, conscientious school teachers sigh in despair as they struggle to promote the virtue of hard work and academic qualifications. Many young people actually end up stumbling into any kind of job, as they find themselves forced to join the rat race - with any dreams they might have once had quickly forgotten. Some merely settle for becoming part of the long-term unemployed.

Whereas technology has unquestionably advanced in recent decades, education has sadly stagnated and fallen well short of any ideal. We are failing the next generations and society in general. Mediocrity

***Above:** Working at Komsberg, non-paid, erecting mile after mile of perimeter fencing is a world away from the life of a footballer's wife or girlfriend.*

remains the norm, with a poverty of aspiration commonplace. What I know and am talking about is therefore way beyond most people's everyday thinking. There is a culture of unpreparedness.

## ii. Dysfunction

The majority of all suffering is caused by selfishness. The list is long but includes insecurity, self-pity, isolation, greed, the hurtfulness of bitching and gossip, financial debt, hatred, prejudice, comfort eating and obesity, anorexia and bulimia, depression, envy, boredom, alcohol and drug abuse, self-loathing and self-harm, anxiety, and much more on a personal level. Then there are the major crimes such as murder, rape, child abuse, robbery and theft, fraud, kidnapping, arson, drink driving, vandalism, assault, drug dealing and trafficking, blackmail, domestic violence, etc. Finally, the global problems include war, over-population, habitat destruction, extinction of species, climate change, pollution, absolute poverty and hunger, terrorism, cruelty to animals, torture, sexual and racial discrimination, genocide, and more. What we do to others, to ourselves, to domesticated animals, and to wildlife and the environment is disgraceful. All of this suffering is completely unnecessary.

Such widespread distress or dysfunctional behaviour provides a compelling reason for change. Almost everyone knows it is wrong - yet bizarrely it is more or less tolerated, as if we are incapable of action to the contrary. One of the common responses is just to keep your head down; "I'm alright, Jack". Until you're not, then you cry for help. Many deny personal responsibility, not even bothering to think.

I don't consider the human race to be truly civilized. We are intelligent, yet lack the wisdom to properly use what knowledge we have so far gained. I sometimes wonder what an advanced extraterrestrial civilization would think of us. They surely wouldn't be stupid enough to consider landing on the proverbial White House lawn any time soon; we're still too backward. So we need a better perspective. We need to grow up through developing a healthier psychology.

*"And pray that there's intelligent life somewhere up in space 'cause there's bugger all down here on Earth."*

*Galaxy Song*
Monty Python

## iii. Failure and false expectation

It would be naive to expect that a solution might come from any of the following: religion, politics, philosophy, economics, or technology. The first three on the list have already had more than ample time to deliver.....and haven't. So why should the situation radically change now?

The world's major religions are not new. Christianity has had just over 2,000 years to prove itself. Buddhism is a bit older still and Islam slightly less so. Hinduism has been around for much longer than the rest. The teachings all contain excellent advice, pointing the way to a better way of living. Yet seven billion people remain in the same old selfish mindset.

How long is enough? Alexander Graham Bell invented the telephone just over a hundred years ago. It has since been developed further into the fax machine and the cordless phone. More recently, we have seen the birth of the mobile or cellular phone - a device that

*Above: There is cruelty to animals, as well as widespread dysfunction within our own species.*

nowadays can also take photographs, play music, access information, and so on. This example of the telephone proves that we are capable of intelligent understanding, development, and application. So surely two thousand years or thereabouts is more than enough time to get to grips with something much more important and beneficial than the telephone?

Various political systems have also promised much. The world has seen everything from communism to capitalism, democracy to auto-cracy or dictatorship - as well as imperialism, monarchy, theocracy, socialism, and fascism. Yet the countless instances of suffering continue. I guess most of us would look to democracy as the best of the bunch. The problem is that democracy requires the popular or majority vote and so is unlikely to lead the people with radical reform. And, anyway, how many people bother to fully understand the complex issues of what they're voting for? Furthermore, where are the suitable political candidates worthy of our votes? (I am reminded of a badge that was worn by some of us during the elections of the mid 1970s: "Don't vote. You might encourage them!")

Philosophers down the ages have made a difference to how we think. Famous names include Plato, Aristotle, Confucius, Lao Tsu, Thomas Aquinas, Rene Descartes, Francis Bacon, Immanuel Kant, and William James to list just a few. Many others are less well-known. Today, philosophy is taught and studied in universities all over the world. But to what effect? Do the philosophy students themselves, once graduated, become outstanding citizens?

Economic strategy provides yet another model for change. Absol-ute poverty restricts the opportunity for choice - whereas the creation of wealth opens up a host of possibilities as well as alleviating one level of suffering. The "I want more" or "I deserve it" dream is sold to us almost everywhere we look. Advertising is big business. And it works. If you aren't prepared to take control of your own mind and what you want to do with your life, then the bombardment of adverts for this-that-and-the-other will persuade you what you should be wanting. Companies don't waste huge amounts of money on mass advertising for nothing; they know how to influence you to buy their products, willingly aided by the latest style icons. However, research

*"A man has free choice to the extent that he is rational."*

Thomas Aquinas

*"Money is like manure. Of very little use except it be spread."*

Francis Bacon

**Far left:** *A polluted river in Kathmandu, Nepal.*

*Above: Vultures play an important part in their ecosystem. But a similar "grab and go" behaviour in humans should be questioned.*

has repeatedly shown that levels of happiness do not rise beyond a certain point in line with increased wealth or material affluence; money helps, but not beyond what might be called "sufficient".

We have all started to see the effects of greed and overspending - be it on a personal, corporate, national, or international level. Riots and mass protests flare-up when the cracks in the promised economic miracle appear. Some want something for nothing; others object to austerity measures, even when national deficits are ludicrously high. Obscene amounts of debt are normalised and the lust of "I want more" continues. Globalisation still has not peaked. What will happen when the man or woman employed in a Chinese factory, currently working for one tenth of the money demanded by the British equivalent, wants equality? The economic bubble, at some point, will burst.

Finally, can technology possibly offer an overall solution? Techno-logical advances have certainly made an impact in some areas, such as improved health care and a reduction in pollution. And information has become more widely available as a result of such innovation.

Worldwide travel and long-distance communication are now common-place. There are endless opportunities for freedom of expression - from driving fast cars and jet skis, to playing on game consoles and singing along with karaoke machines. Manufactured drugs, legal or illegal, can either temporarily numb the pain of depression or else provide an artificial short-term high. That said, technology seems unlikely to develop any kind of a permanent solution to the basic issue of the human race being "flawed".

# iv. Psychology

As an academic discipline, psychology has struggled to find its feet. It has always been in the shadow of the three great pillars of science; biology, physics, and chemistry have reigned supreme as the main no-nonsense subjects, dealing with physical realities. By comparison, psychology has been seen as somewhat vague, as it deals with "the mind". The best psychologists work to build a reliable body of knowledge, rigorously supported by data. Neuroscience offers psychology valuable corroboration, as we increase our understanding of how the brain functions.

> *"Habits of thinking need not be forever."*
>
> Martin Seligman

Martin Seligman was elected President of the American Psychological Association in 1998 by the widest margin in its history. He has summarised the state of psychology today as "not good enough". His career has mostly been spent working in the area of mental illness and he makes the point that, after a "fuzzy" start, professionals have only discovered how to treat a handful of pathological conditions in the past 60 years or so. (Antipsychotic drugs can treat schizophrenia, for example, whilst cognitive therapy can help people overcome phobias such as a fear of flying.) Psychology meanwhile forgot about improving normal lives and those with exceptional ability. Seligman now argues that psychology should be as concerned with strengths as weaknesses - helping to build the best, instead of just repairing the worst. He goes further, stating that well-being comes from exercising kindness or altruism - more readily than it does from just having fun. In other words, the evidence demonstrates that a life of meaning and purpose is more fulfilling than one spent trying to get as much pleasure as possible.

Psychology will eventually catch up with and champion the considerable benefits that I am describing in this book. Abraham Maslow (1908-1970) showed early promise by examining what he called peak experiences and self-actualisation - although he is better remembered for his hierarchy of needs theory. Two extracts from Maslow's work make clear his thinking:

> *"The story of the human race is the story of men and women selling themselves short."*
>
> Abraham Maslow

> *"Certainly a visitor from Mars descending upon a colony of birth-injured cripples, dwarfs, [and] hunchbacks...could not deduce what they should have been. But then let us not study cripples, but the closest thing we can get to whole, healthy men. In them, we find qualitative differences, a different system of motivation, emotion, value, thinking, and perceiving. In a certain sense, only the saints are mankind. All the rest are cripples."*

And again:

> *"The notion I am working towards is of some ideal of human nature, closely approximated in reality by a few 'self-actualised' people. Everybody else is sick [to] a greater or lesser degree, it is true, but these degrees are much less important than we have thought. There seems no intrinsic reason why everyone shouldn't be this way [i.e. self-actualised]. Apparently, every baby has possibilities for self-actualisation, but most get it knocked out of them.*
>
> *"I think of the self-actualising man not as an ordinary man with something added, but rather as the ordinary man with nothing taken away."*

Richard Maurice Bucke (1837-1902) is less well-known but was one of the leading psychiatrists of his time. In addition to eminent positions held in Canada, he was also President of the Psychological Section of the British Medical Association - as well as President of the American Medico-Psychological Association. Following a sudden and illuminating experience of his own at the age of 36, Bucke studied others who had similar experiences or glimpses of what he termed

"cosmic consciousness". His work is considered to be the first academic analysis of what are now more commonly called unity, peak, mystical, or oneness experiences.

Transpersonal psychology has more recently made an attempt to advance the study and application of these issues, but has struggled to gain ground. It remains at the fringes of mainstream psychology. Perhaps the psychologists' own levels of understanding has been a limiting factor. I would also suggest there has been a miscalculation regarding the importance of avoidance as a central factor of psychological behaviour.

It is crucial that psychology - supported by neuroscience - sooner or later thoroughly evaluates all aspects of human potential, because an evidence-based approach is essential. And, educationally, the subject must be de-mystified.

*Above: Sipapu natural bridge in Utah. Despite its 220ft height and enormous 268ft span, it isn't immediately obvious and can be hard to spot from the overlook on the canyon rim.*

# 3

# Khawaja

## i. Famine

Seeing the famine in Ethiopia in January 1985 with my own eyes was deeply moving. The countless deaths were unnecessary. Addis Ababa was only six and a half flying hours away from London, Heathrow. Ethiopia wasn't some place on a distant planet. Equally shocking was the attitude of the various international aid agencies I encountered.

We helped several thousand people in the relief camps around Makelle, Tigray, by distributing blankets we had air-lifted. The nights were bitterly cold in the Ethiopian Highlands, often proving to be too much for the children whose bodies had already been weakened by famine and illness. Something as basic as a blanket could literally make the difference between life and death. A lot of people were being temporarily sheltered in tents. However, thousands of others were still living outside - having left their villages and walked for days or weeks in hope of finding food aid. They were doing what they could, huddled in small depressions behind low stone walls for protection against the cold winds. We distributed the majority of our blankets to these families - the most desperately in need.

If you look at the two photographs on the opposite page and below, you'll notice a few white tents in the background. There were

*Right and far right:* Famine in
Ethiopia, January 1985. Something as
basic as a blanket could literally make
the difference between life and death.

36

*Above: Before and after. They didn't have much.*

actually more tents than these photos show. I was seeing them, day after day, as we worked hard to help the people. But what I couldn't understand was why these particular tents were being left empty, so I eventually went to ask the Italian aid agency staff in charge what was happening. Their attitude could be summed up as a mixture of apathy, incompetence, and disconnectedness. When I then challenged them - pointing out that their neglect was costing lives - they retaliated by accusing me of "meddling" in "their" affairs. It was unbelievable, yet I saw similar behaviour over and over again.

This was originally intended as a "one-off" relief trip, but once in Ethiopia it became obvious we had to do more. Initially, I considered channelling any future help through the usual aid organisations. After being shown three of the relief camps situated around the town of Makelle, together with the field director of one of the best-known British charities, I offered him our help. "Give me a shopping list of anything that's needed, costing at least £50,000, and I'll deliver it

wherever you want within the next few months." He replied "I don't know what to do with the £6,000,000 I've already got." He said this to me as he was eating his lunch, also admitting he was "the wrong man for the job".

On another occasion during this first field trip, I worked with an excellent Ethiopian nurse, bringing those who were seriously ill to her for medical help. She was employed by a Japanese aid agency and they had set up a hospital tent at one of the camps. When I carried the first patient to this facility, the Ethiopian nurse greeted me by saying "Sorry, we are full." But as the canvas beds inside were all empty, I proceeded and she quickly responded. We made a good team and the hospital tent soon filled up. Later that day, I asked the British field director (just mentioned) what was going on. He told me that the two Japanese doctors in charge were also the wrong people for the job. This was clarified when I saw them myself the next day. They briefly turned up for an hour or two, covered from head to toe;

*Above:* The British Royal Air Force helped us. Unlike the aid agencies, they were professional and efficient.

39

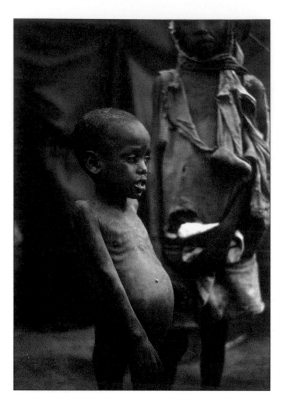

*Above (left):*
*Malnourishment was still bad on our return.*

*Above (right):*
*The northern Ethiopians showed considerable dignity, even when faced with the most desperate hardship.*

each was wearing a face mask, white coat, surgical gloves, and wellington boots. They seemed paralysed in their inactivity, clearly terrified by the risk of getting ill themselves. Rather than returning to Japan, asking to be replaced by individuals more suited to this challenging emergency situation in East Africa, perhaps the wish to maintain face was even stronger and so they remained.

## ii.  Back again

A few months later, we were back in Ethiopia again - this time with three airplane loads of relief and development supplies - as the famine continued. A religious Scandinavian aid organisation was working in the same locality. Five foreign nurses had five brand new four-wheel-drive vehicles - i.e. one each - yet only a small amount of two medical drugs available. Someone had made a serious miscalculation, clearly

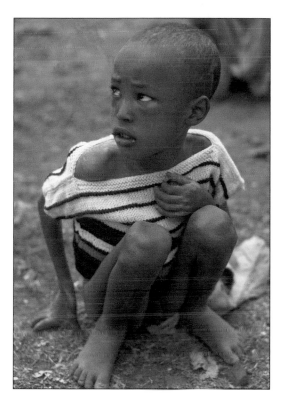

getting the priorities wrong. The Scandinavian nurse that I first met was lovely and I immediately offered to share some of our medical supplies. We had brought lots of the World Health Organisation's emergency list of 22 essential drugs, etc - enough for tens of thousands of patients. She was delighted by the offer but said she should first check with her colleagues. Amazingly, the four other foreign nurses refused any of our medical supplies and she went along with their "decision".

We were, however, invited to supper. It would be fair to say that the three of us were surprised at the extravagence of the five-course meal on offer. During supper, it emerged that they had also run out of milk powder to distribute to those most in need. We had loads with us and again offered to co-operate. They willingly accepted on this occasion, seemingly blind to the glaring inconsistency. Whilst they drank coffee - dipping in high-energy biscuits specially designed for malnourished children - one of the nurses further explained they

*Above: We took thousands of knitted woollen tops for the young children on our second trip that helped keep them warm.*

41

also had a shortage of these same high-energy biscuits. At this point, I hastily said our goodnights, just in time to prevent one of my colleagues from lashing out; she was understandably incensed by their hypocrisy.

The day before returning back to the UK, I travelled to a different region, then known as Wollo Province, in a Polish Air Force helicopter. There, in a remote village and with almost no supplies remaining, a 15-year-old Ethiopian girl died in my arms. She had severe diarrhoea and I could have almost certainly saved her life if I had had just a few pence worth of medicine with me. This was another senseless death. Otherwise helpless, I promised never to forget her and to this day her memory serves as a reminder to our own charity work to never waste money.

> *"We can't go on pretending day by day that someone somewhere will soon make a change."*
>
> We Are The World
> USA for Africa

## iii. Development

Soon afterwards, we began a long-term development project in Sudan. The government authorities gave us responsibility for the medical care of 3,500 Ethiopian and Eritrean refugees at the Awad el Sid camp - plus tens of thousands of poor Sudanese villagers in the surrounding area.

Over the next 25 years, our medical clinic examined, diagnosed, and treated between 25,000 and 35,000 patients each year. In total, we helped approximately 750,000 patients. We first built and worked from a handful of tukels - thatched mud huts - later progressing to brick buildings. I made sure that our medical stocks never ran out and we quickly established a reputation for consistency and service before self. Occasional patients even travelled to us from Khartoum, much to my surprise, which was at least a day's journey away.

In addition to the main focus of our medical work, we set up sewing and carpentry workshops. We also encouraged tree planting and vegetable growing. And we provided education to children and adults. Later, we started our own forest for timber production and income generation, plus a dairy cow herd to provide milk and extra income. Furthermore, adjoining our clinic compound, we purchased land to start Sudan's first private nature reserve. The British government

*Above:* Awad el Sid

funded us for more years than they should have, quietly telling us that we provided the best value for money they had ever known. And we were proud to be the only non-Christian project given funding by a Christian charity for 24 years.

The Sudanese government repeatedly told us we were "the best", urging us to reproduce the clinic all over the country. We declined to do so, reminding them that 56 other international aid organisations also worked in Sudan under their supervision. They increasingly took notice of how we were different and made a number of changes in overseeing the other agencies as a result.

Meanwhile, we had carried out a confidential investigation of non-government and UN organisations in six other countries - Ethiopia, Uganda, Somalia, India, Bangladesh, and Nepal - over a seven and a half month period. We interviewed hundreds of field staff (expatriate and local) and visited numerous project sites. The ineffectiveness and inefficiency of aid agencies was widespread and much worse than I had initially seen in Ethiopia during the famine. Our findings were

> *"...an excellent analysis of what can and will go wrong in so many NGO projects.....a wonderful resource tool."*
>
> NGO Chief Executive

*Above: The clinic at Awad el Sid opens. One tukel (mud hut) was used for examinations, another for treatment, yet another as a laboratory, and a fourth stored our supply of medical drugs.*
*We hadn't yet covered the outside of the tukel with a layer of mud and donkey dung in the photograph above, so it must have been taken in the first couple of days. Numbers of patients quickly increased.*

compiled into a report which was sent to the heads of the various charities, UN agencies, and governments. Some massively appreciated our straightforward efforts - but I'm sure that others probably wanted to bury the report as quickly as possible. We deliberately omitted names of individuals and organisations to protect anonymity, allowing greater openness and trust during the investigation stage.

Aid agencies generally exaggerate the amount of good they do and gloss over their many failings. International aid has become "big business" and huge amounts of money are involved. Empire building, flag flying, and competitiveness are rife. Misuse is compounded by corruption. Staff wages are generous. Ask the employees of five-star hotels in the capital city of any least developed country what they think of aid organisations and the answer will likely be the same: "Big salary. Big office. Big car."

Clever report writing and intelligent-sounding jargon hides a mass of practical incompetence. The world of aid agency staff is usually far apart from the realities of being poor. Racial and religious prejudice

is common. The wrong kind of aid is often provided and the expression "too little, too late" is very appropriate. Misfits easily find a job and gain promotion, as there is no commercial pressure to show results and failure is quickly forgotten or outright ignored.

*Above: Years later, the tukels were replaced with brick buildings.*

Field visits by management are too short. Red carpet visits for VIPs are little more than a public relations exercise. Project evaluation becomes meaningless without honesty and thoroughness. Ladder-climbing career prospects encourages compliance, so any rocking of the proverbial boat is a rarity. Funding grants follow fashionable theories. (We were once refused a grant because we offered medical care for everyone - children, women, and men - instead of just women.)

The scale of misspending is huge. Find out for yourself how much the director of a typical aid charity or UN organisation is paid each year - then compare this to the heart-pulling adverts and appeals for your donation of £3 each month. And this is just the tip of the iceberg. During a meeting at the Sudanese Embassy in London years ago, a senior member of staff told me he had formerly worked for a well-

*Above (left and right):*
*This little boy's father couldn't understand why his son didn't walk, believing that Allah was punishing him. We then diagnosed cerebral palsy. Step by step, our nurses got the youngster walking and the father became proud of his son.*

*Right:* *This patient's leg had to be amputated. The stump then required dressing for many weeks. We later fitted an artificial limb.*

known British charity as their accountant within Sudan. This came out when we were discussing the aid game and I had said that at least 1% of the money gets through and is spent correctly. He strongly disagreed, insisting it was much less than 1% - backing up his statement with detail after detail, typical of a trained accountant. And the charity he worked for? It's the one I MOST admire, if not in terms of how they spend their funding.....

Nationals in the various developing countries are commonly upset by the gross ineffectiveness and inefficiency of aid organisations. It is their people, after all, who remain poor - despite the billions of dollars available "to help" every year. But they are voiceless in the rich developed countries. A senior Sudanese government official in Khartoum once told me that I might be a khawaja (white man or foreigner) on the outside, but I was really Sudanese on the inside.

# 4

# Progress

## i. Prompted

Ranthambhore tiger reserve in India was in crisis. Many of the famous tigers of the 1980s had been recently killed by poachers. The story made headline news around the world, including here in the UK. This was January 1994 and, by coincidence, we were scheduled to be working in and around Ranthambhore at the same time. By then, we unusually had considerable hands-on experience in both nature conservation and village development - ideal for looking at practical ways to minimise wildlife-human conflict.

In addition to various meetings in Delhi, we spent an intensive ten days at Ranthambhore. We always started early in the morning and worked late into the night, making best use of every minute and hour. We questioned and listened to the government department staff, from forest guards to the field director. We met with villagers, including those doing illegal wood-cutting and livestock grazing. We interviewed hotel owners and staff, as well as vehicle drivers and guides who looked after tourists. Furthermore, we met with representatives of several non-government organisations working in the area. We discussed everything with Fateh Singh Rathore, the original

*Right: Fateh Singh Rathore.*

*Far right: Poaching, together with habitat loss, is threatening the tiger with extinction.*

*"Here we go again...
There's so much that
we need to share."*

*Give A Little Bit*
Supertramp

field director of Ranthambhore whose conviction and work resulted in the tigers flourishing during those earlier years - and also with Valmik Thapar, author and documentary presenter, and energetic campaigner, who had already spent a chunk of his life trying to save the tiger. We even interviewed a poacher in jail, recently caught in the act.

It was our last full day at Ranthambhore and, by mid-morning, a change of circumstance suggested we should spend the late afternoon inside the reserve. So I went back to the government offices to get permission. I went to see Yogesh Kumar Sahu, assistant field director of Ranthambhore. We had had a long meeting with him just two days earlier. Before he attended to my request, Yogesh Sahu confronted me: "You're enlightened, aren't you?"

I was somewhat surprised, having effectively kept quiet for over a decade about what had happened to me. And there was no room for manoeuvre as he repeatedly insisted that I had to be. He was familiar with a constant stream of international experts coming to Ranthambhore, some of them staying as long as six months. But he had never known anyone grasp all the complexities as I had, based on our previous meeting, and in just over a week. Yogesh Sahu maintained that only an enlightened mind could satisfactorily explain my behaviour. I admitted he was correct, before leaving with permission for entry to the reserve. Initially mentored by Fateh Singh, he was no fool - and Yogesh Sahu's deduction prompted me to re-think. Before midnight, I had decided that it was time to talk out again about what I knew of human potential.....

## ii. Building a team

By March 1994, I had written *Human Potential - the search for that "something more"*. This was followed in 1996 with another book called *Actions Speak Louder Than Words*. I initially discussed the subject with a number of leading academics interested in consciousness change. They were knowledgeable and helpful but hadn't really thought about things as practically as myself. We also tried to arrange a research

project, involving several universities and respected professionals in various fields, in co-operation with another organisation and their membership. However, the proposed arrangements looked likely to fall short of the high levels that I considered necessary, so we reluctantly pulled out during the planning phase. The Human Potential Trust has the legal aim of research, incidentally, in addition to the main objective of providing education on this subject.

Gradually, we built up a small team of just over a dozen or so individuals interested in changing themselves and improving things around them. They became practically involved at The Oasis nature reserve and education centre, usually working there two days each week, as well as fundraising for our on-going work in Sudan. Plus, we talked about the human potential issues - including what usually frustrates change or progress. By 1998, the team had become established, hard working, and capable. In the spring of the same year, we purchased a few acres of adjoining semi-natural ancient woodland, conveniently named Oasis Woods. This came up for auction and the

*Above:* A gravel bed in
*The Oasis Gardens.*

*Above:*
*Crocosmia 'Lucifer'*
*adds vibrant colour in*
*The Oasis Gardens.*

woodland attracted a lot of attention; the bidding was fierce and the price accordingly escalated. The Wildlife For All Trust didn't have much finance available at the time, but my colleague Jonathan had some inheritance money and generously offered to boost our funds. A couple of other team members added what they could to the pot. Thankfully, at the end of the bidding, Oasis Woods was ours - now a part of The Oasis. Our land is situated within an Area of Outstanding Natural Beauty.

Jonathan, a pharmacist with a degree in psychology, has recently written on our website as follows:

> *"The word 'unique' is used a lot, often without really meaning very much. In the case of Wildlife For All, however, it is very appropriate. Not just because we are 'different', but because we are different in ways which are exceptional. I have seen a number of people get involved over the years, most of whom (including myself) were pretty average. Within a relatively short time, many of these very ordinary*

*individuals were achieving far more than they would have thought they were capable of. I was someone who was riddled with apathy and yet, because of Wildlife For All's unique way of working, soon found myself genuinely making a difference."*

Deliberately doing this work non-paid, and financially supporting ourselves with other work, we were strongly achievement-orientated. Our project in South Africa to safeguard the critically endangered geometric tortoise was started back in 1992. It further developed when we set up The Tortoise Farm nature reserve in 2001, thanks to the generous support of a farmer who gave us 69 acres of suitable habitat. Soon afterwards, in 2002, we purchased a 16,000 acre sheep farm in another part of South Africa to establish Komsberg Wilderness Nature Reserve. Situated within both the upland succulent Karoo and fynbos biomes - widely recognised as two of the world's 25 most important conservation hotspots for biodiversity - Komsberg is a huge place. The sense of wilderness is authentic and truly awesome. And the amount of hard work,

*Above:*
*Hemerocallis*
*'Lady Neva' (left) and*
*'Prince of Purple' (right)*
*are two of our more*
*spectacular plants.*

*Above:* The mountains
you can see in this
photograph are just a
small part of Komsberg.
It is a huge place.

determination, and dedication needed to do everything was tremendous. Then, in 2006, we bought an adjoining property, thereby effectively
doubling Komsberg's size to its present 30,700 acres or 125 sq km. It is
one of the biggest private nature reserves in South Africa.

Komsberg means "surrounded by mountains" and the reserve has
three different types of habitat. We have numerous mountains and
mountainsides, plus extensive mountain plateau offering good grazing
for wildlife, and finally a lower valley area 2,400ft or 730m below
with thousands of acacias and other trees. Several dramatic overlook
points provide excellent views of this spectacular scenery. And it has
taken years of phenomenal effort to get Komsberg to how it is today
.....and this hard work continues.

The removal of miles and miles of internal camp fencing is necessary
so that the larger animals can roam freely. This task alone would be
challenging, but it was just the beginning. Lorry loads of perimeter
fencing materials have had to be bought at considerable cost, off-loaded,

carried into position up and down mountains, and then finally erected to a height of 2.4m. Our boundary fence is 98km or 61 miles in length (excluding what we have put up, then later taken down after the reserve was extended). Gates have needed to be made and waterholes adapted from sheep use to wildlife. Roads must be repaired after thunderstorms and regular boundary checks are essential so as to maintain a secure perimeter fence.

*Above: One of several dramatic overlook points. Our main homestead is in the distance below.*

## iii. Aim

As important as it is to protect threatened habitats and conserve endangered species, or help the poorest of the poor, the human potential aim is the key to ending the otherwise endless suffering that is so widespread in our world. What has happened to me is not really a start. I may provide an opportunity for others to learn, but if this urgently-needed learning doesn't actually occur then there is no beginning or movement forward. I would die an oddity, having failed, with the worms and micro-organisms unlikely to appreciate that the brain they were devouring was once different.

So my aim has been to teach how to make life better. Specifically, I have identified the need to establish an example of a few individual role models who would be worthy of consideration by others. A dozen or so men and women has been my goal, as this should be sufficient to kick-start the process leading to a wider change. I briefly mentioned this in *Actions Speak Louder Than Words* and wrote as follows:

> *"Excellence and integrity should characterise this multiple example. Individuals must be independently-minded, yet freely willing to work together. They each need to demonstrate a balanced competence. The ability to think more, care more, and do more must be developed in a combined manner. Anything less than an 80% shift - where 0% is normal consciousness and 100% is complete non-selfishness - would be unsuitable as part of this suggested example. Whereas it does not have to be perfect, a high degree of contrast is required to signify the non-selfish alternative."*

An 80% shift in behaviour would probably be enough to inspire and guide a few more people to then do the same. I guess that two or three of these pioneers would then, sooner or later, have the inclination to try to go all the way. One quality needed is what I call "the spirit of an adventurer" - and I hope this attribute would eventually help develop everything to the logical conclusion. Together, they ought to be able to work out the final few steps. I have already provided a few written words of advice in my books on the need for a "spinning-top effect" that might be helpful in such a final push. (This might happen whilst I am still alive, but I don't consider it to be a crucial part of what I need to help establish during my lifetime.) I am deliberately running ahead of the story again here, but it is important to explain the aim - and I'm going to carry on for a bit longer.

The conditioning effect of the human race on each other is strong. Therefore, change is difficult to achieve. The effects of avoidance

*"Waiting here for everyman."*

For Everyman
Jackson Browne

include self-deception and the scale is undoubtedly underestimated. After several thousand years of interest in this matter, I do not believe a proper educational breakthrough has yet been demonstrated. The realistic way forward is to first produce a small multi-person example, as I have said above. This must then remain active for some time, without any deterioration in quality, as more role models emerge.

It would probably take several hundred years before the majority of people then belatedly decided that normal selfishness is outdated and counter-productive. I don't like using long words, but this rate of growth or change can be best described as exponential. In other words, very slow or seemingly little progress for a long time - followed by a pronounced upturn or rapid uptake.

*Above: The martial eagle is one of five eagle species found at Komsberg.*

57

*Above: Wussy and Vicky replacing the heavy tail of a windmill.*

*"I was warned as a child of thirteen not to act too strong. Try to look like you belong but don't push girl. I was raised in a no-you-don't world, overrun with rules."*

*Woman in the Moon*
Barbra Streisand

## iv. Limits

One of our core principles is the need to go beyond the supposed-to-be limits. The majority of people too readily accept these conditioned constraints, which are commonly reinforced through disappointment and rejection. When challenged, many will even justify or argue for their limitations. Our team learnt how to exceed these self-imposed restrictions and our significant practical achievements demonstrated this, as already outlined.

Self-centredness has to be overcome. But developing an ability to get off yourself is easier said than done, especially when you appreciate that this normalised state of "me, me, me" tends to be self-perpetuating. Part of knowing how to break the mould is learning how to focus on something bigger or more important than yourself. Many people first experience such a shift - albeit to a small extent - when they become parents; vulnerable babies and dependent infants demand attention.

On a bigger scale, the old-fashioned term "service before self" nicely summarises what is actually required. Albert Einstein provides further understanding:

> *"A human being is a part of the whole, called by us 'universe', a part limited in time and space. We experience ourselves, our thoughts and feelings, as something separate from the rest - a kind of optical delusion of consciousness. This delusion is a prison for us, restricting us to our personal desires and to affection for a few persons nearest to us. Our task must be to free ourselves from this prison by widening our circle of compassion to embrace all living creatures, and the whole of nature in its beauty."*

My ex-wife, Sarah, was raped by a stranger at the age of 10. She wrote about this in the introduction to *Actions Speak Louder Than Words*. During the early part of our 20 years together, she overcame the effects of her childhood trauma. Sarah learnt to go beyond her self-protection barriers by caring about the endangered Australian wallabies we were helping to conserve at that time - more than about herself or, rather, her blocks. She learnt to give, instead of hiding away and playing the clown. In one instance, we needed to acquire a set of mobile exhibition boards for our education work. Sarah eventually persuaded the managing director of the top company to give the boards to us free-of-charge. When we later met him, the managing director was so impressed that he offered Sarah a job as one of his sales staff. She blurted out "Sorry, no, because I couldn't care about your products." I quickly added "as much", clarifying that Sarah was committed to helping endangered wildlife.

Each team member gradually developed a good understanding of psychology, including an ability for self-honesty. The concept of "need before want" became clearer and there was a tremendous willingness to do whatever was needed. Yes, we achieved a lot - but the team also thought a lot too. Several other people expressed an interest in joining us over these years, but didn't always succeed in doing so because self-interests proved more compelling. Our policy of "actions speak louder than words" always sorted out the dreamers from those willing to actually live the dream.

> *"Focusing your life solely on making a buck shows a certain poverty of ambition. It asks too little of yourself. Because it's only when you hitch your wagon to something larger than yourself that you realise your true potential."*
>
> Barack Obama

After a period of approximately ten years, complacency gradually set in. Almost everyone now seemed content to stay at the same level they had already attained. Yet they knew that a number of individual weaknesses clearly remained. These repeatedly showed up as minor problems in the otherwise smooth-running of our project work. Actions speak louder than words, deliberately employed as an anti-hypocrisy test, was still delivering.

Vicky has been involved for over 15 years at this time of writing and comments as follows:

> "The old team delivered exceptional results. We each learnt a deep responsibility that brings with it a profound level of seriousness and commitment, which in turn switches on a hunger for ruthless self-honesty. This level of self-honesty is critical to sort out one's issues.
>
> "The complacency that set in after a number of years resulted in a self-imposed ceiling. It was very subtly encouraged by other team members, usually in unspoken form, as a way to preserve their own ceiling from being overly challenged. We still had moments of insight and some kind of resolve to break through. Everyone's comfort zone bubble was constantly being pricked, but not enough to burst that bubble. Although a hard work ethic prevailed, team members some-times chose to ignore aspects of the training to do with pushing one's potential and applying an on-going attitude of learning.
>
> "We were content with the success of our projects and being part of it all. But what was required was an even deeper seriousness and a greater responsibility for making this pioneering psychological work ultimately succeed. No one, except for Becky (and obviously Iain), was prepared to take full responsibility for the development of the work."

So the team - with the sole exception of Becky, whom I'll mention in more detail in Chapter 6 - got effectively stuck. Individually, most had shifted to about 50% or 60% of what I know to be achievable. Whereas it would be wrong to dismiss such progress, it certainly wasn't mission accomplished. I maintained that nothing less than an 80% shift or more would do. We all talked about this, over and over and over again. But most team members still remained stuck.

*"Nobody said
it was easy.
It's such a shame
for us to part.
Nobody said
it was easy.
No one ever said
it would be so hard.
I'm going back
to the start."*

The Scientist
Coldplay

*Above:* Vicky carrying a
load of cleared deadwood
at The Tortoise Farm.

As it became increasingly obvious that further change was needed, but not happening nor likely to happen, something had to give. Unfortunately, the overall team had to be reduced and then re-built. So over the next three or four years, half a dozen long-serving colleagues left, together with a few who were less experienced. Another departed unexpectedly due to different reasons. I would like to stress that most had done well, contributing much. Some had started with little ability and perhaps had too much baggage. In retrospect, they were probably not the best candidates for such an important pioneering attempt. That they did as well as they did, was itself encouraging.

# 5

# Hurdles

## i. Delusion

The talk after mine was called "Angels, angels, angels" and it was sold out. My talk beforehand was reasonably well attended. But with over a hundred seats still empty in the large lecture room, it was nowhere near full to capacity. This was 1994 and I had been invited to speak at the Mind Body Spirit Festival in London. About 20 minutes before the talk began, the event's deputy organiser asked me how I wanted to be introduced to the audience. I was initially unsure what he was saying, because brief details had already been printed in their programme, until he elaborated by saying that mine was the only lecture or workshop in the whole week that was genuinely educational - adding that all the rest were superficial entertainment or nonsense. I liked his frankness. As this was the only talk I have ever agreed to do involving an entry fee - the money was going directly to our charity work, not myself - I replied by asking him to inform everyone attending that as I was about to be bluntly honest, an immediate refund was available if anyone wanted to leave. They all stayed.

Fifteen years before, I had quietly gone along to the same event at the request of someone who knew me. Whilst there, I coined the term "spiritual circus". And here lies the first hurdle for those searching

*Right and far right:*
*The wolf is seen by some as having "special powers".*

for that "something more". There is a mess of so-called "alternatives" on offer, often amounting to little more than mumbo-jumbo. And it is frequently exploitative. People amazingly lap it up, however, playing at being "different".

I will undoubtedly alienate some readers by criticising this mess of "alternatives", but this issue is a major stumbling block as people can easily get hijacked, side-tracked, or perhaps simply be put off by such gross stupidity. A few spiritually-minded souls will gently tell me that sorting out the wheat from the chaff is part of searching and that people do progress. It is, however, chaff city and any advancement will merely be deeper into that place where the sun doesn't shine. Rejecting a belief in tarot cards and then next putting your faith (and money) in crystals or books/talks about guardian angels still seems infantile to me. I once believed in Santa Claus too - and even saw him one Christmas, later being told it was actually my uncle dressed up - but only as a young child.

There is plenty of companionship to be found in all of this fantasy and self-indulgence. It is possible that you might progress to an interest in healing, in which case someone will probably tell you that you have a special gift; intrigued and flattered, and several courses later, you could easily find yourself supposedly healing others. Alternatively, someone else might reveal you are a gifted psychic. You go on to train as a medium or sensitive in the art of channelling, and before long you are telling some recently bereaved stranger that Aunty Jane from beyond the grave has something to say. You probably won't realise that the only thing you have received is coaching in what is known as cold reading; you're basically a good person, not deliberately out to deceive. But the initial spirit of searching can be sabotaged through being gullible. It is easy to believe a load of bullshit. Many people do. And beware of anyone using pseudoscience in a poor attempt to back up their hollow claims.

The area of alternative medicine holds special appeal for many in what is a sick society. Surveys suggest that more than half of the UK population spends money on such "alternatives"; it is big business. (So over half of you reading this book are now definitely going to be upset with me at this point!) In the 1970s, a number of us thought

*"Some of them were dreamers.*
*Some of them were fools.*
*They were making plans and thinking of the future."*

*Before the Deluge*
Jackson Browne

there might be something useful in the traditional Eastern practices that we were hearing about - but they mostly proved to be ineffective. The benefits commonly reported were because of the placebo effect, something which is well-known to conventional medicine and science. Since then, a whole range of iffy and colourful so-called treatments have sprung up, as quickly as weeds in a garden. Many people are easily suckered into passionately believing a load of hot air. Slow to critically question and often ignorant of science, they prefer the buzz of myth and escapism instead of facing hard reality. But, to go back to what I said at the beginning of this paragraph, it is a sad reflection on our sick society. More importantly, it has got nothing whatsoever to do with the real search for that "something more".

The higher forms of spiritual pursuit also seem to encourage self-indulgence. A sub-culture has arisen in the past few decades, once commonly known as the "New Age" movement, perpetuated by a range of dubious groups and dodgy spiritual teachers. It may not be as blatantly crude as the televangelists in America, but such egotistical wallowing is still sickening. The blind are leading the blind in a game of seek and follow. The Westernised use of traditional Eastern truths merely spices up this game, creating an illusion of learning. Meditation, for example, continues to thrive and, when I question its effectiveness, converts get upset that I dare challenge this holy cow. The reality is that techniques like meditation - in its various forms - have been employed by well-meaning seekers of truth in the distant past who had only reached a limited degree of understanding. They were doing their best, but nevertheless groping and fumbling in semi-darkness.

Several individuals have claimed to be enlightened during these past few decades, some of whom are now dead. They could certainly talk the talk, luring plenty of followers, and I do not doubt that they had some level of insight or realisation. However, I could easily tell they were deceiving themselves - and definitely misleading others - simply by what they were NOT saying. Traditional literature rightly warns of such falsehood or pitfall. An egotistical pumped-up male in his late twenties or early thirties, having spent several years compulsively searching, seems especially vulnerable to mistaking a degree of

*"Superstition ain't the way."*

Stevie Wonder

*"You're an idiot, babe. It's a wonder that you still know how to breathe."*

*Idiot Wind*
Bob Dylan

awakening with actual enlightenment. Again, sadly, it is the blind leading the blind - or, more precisely, should I say partially-sighted?

I have deliberately kept away from this mess, focusing on what I know to be essential. The classical use of the term "enlightened" has been cheapened, along with the worthwhile journey of searching for greater awareness. Accordingly, I long ago invented a new word to explain this real potential as simply as possible: non-selfishness. And I have clearly emphasised the need for an anti-hypocrisy test - actions speak louder than words - as a means of counteracting self-deception, which I'll say more about in Chapter 10.

## ii. Myth vs. reality

*"Truth exists.
Only lies
are invented."*

*Georges Braque*

Chief Seattle's inspirational speech has become legendary, repeated on posters, leaflets, magazines, books, DVDs, and websites:

> *"What is man without the beasts? If all the beasts were gone, man would die from a great loneliness of spirit. For whatever happens to the beasts, soon happens to man. All things are connected. Man did not weave the web of life; he is merely a strand in it. Whatever he does to the web, he does to himself."*

The reality, however, is different from the myth. There was a real Chief Seattle. But the speech is fictional - the words of a scriptwriter called Ted Perry from a 1971 film. In its first limited showing, the speech was clearly accredited to Perry. Producers subsequently revised Perry's script and removed the credit line without his knowledge when the film was re-shown on one of the television networks. Viewers requested a transcript of the inspirational speech and 18,000 posters were sent out in quick response.

Parts of the speech are historically inaccurate. For example:

> *"I have seen a thousand rotting buffaloes on the prairies left by the white man who shot them from a passing train."*

There were no buffalo anywhere near the Chief's tribal homeland; he lived a thousand miles from the prairies. And Chief Seattle's days

*Above:* Bison (also known as buffalo) in Yellowstone.

were before the Union and Central Pacific railroads had been built across the prairies. Ted Perry has honestly admitted such historical bloomers as "pure ignorance on my part" and he tried to set the record straight about his fictitious writings, adding "On reflection, it was ethically wrong." But the myth had already taken on a life of its own. Friends of the Earth have repeatedly used the "speech". Al Gore, US vice-president, referred to Chief Seattle in his book on the environment. Dan Fogelberg, one of my favourite singer/songwriters of all time, included some of the inspirational words within the packaging of one of his CDs.

If you are one of those who respond by saying "But does it really matter?", my answer is a definite "yes". First of all, I doubt that Fred the toilet cleaner saying exactly the same words would have had the same va-va-voom or je ne sais quoi appeal. Secondly, there is a real danger of mislearning if lots of people have a predisposition towards what is hopeful but merely mythical, rather than a tendency for established fact.

*Above: Lamar Valley is part of Yellowstone's vast wilderness.*

The same inclination shows up in some people's attitude towards dolphins. Spiritual aspirations are attributed to these charming sea creatures, exaggerating what is true. We are urged to believe dolphins are "pure" and that they can "inspire and uplift us" - and even "the dolphins want many dolphin energy healers sharing this very special healing energy around the planet." Marine biologists, supported by physicists, would rightly challenge the existence of such "dolphin healing energy". But the knock-out blow surely comes in the form of groups of male dolphins repeatedly gang-raping female dolphins and even other males - as shown on David Attenborough documentary films and well-known to marine biologists. When I have mentioned this undisputed fact to over-the-top dolphin worshippers, they seemingly don't hear. Perhaps they don't want their illusion shattered?

The wolf is another substitute for spiritual wonderment. I took the photographic images at the beginning of this chapter in Yellowstone National Park for my last book, *Holding On*, which included the

success story of restoring wolves to Yellowstone after an absence of 69 years. And the dream of bringing wolves back took over 50 years to realise after it was first recommended in 1944. Opposition from local ranchers and politicians was fierce; irrationally, they labelled the wolf as "the Saddam Hussein of the animal world". The situation certainly wasn't helped when new age supporters began claiming that wolves are "our spiritual brothers and sisters" with "special awareness and other supernatural powers" - and that they "could do no wrong". National Park Service officials, biologists, and mainstream conservationists groaned in dismay at yet another setback.

Eventually, in January 1995, the first wolves arrived. After a period spent in acclimatisation pens, they were given their full freedom of Yellowstone's vast wilderness in late March. In January 1996, wolf #3 wandered beyond the national park and killed a sheep. Recaptured and re-released 60 miles away, it returned to the same ranch and attacked another sheep. Wolf #3 was shot by an official, according to agreed procedure, after this second incident. Another wolf, #27, was likewise officially removed from the project after killing sheep beyond Yellowstone; she simply didn't understand the human concept of artificial boundaries and, being wild and free, paid the ultimate price for just being a wolf. This magnificent predator is a wonder of nature - worthy of our respect and awe - but the outrageous claims of "special powers" are blatantly untrue.

As another example of myth vs. reality, I am again going to risk becoming unpopular with many by challenging the current fad or obsession with organic food and all things natural. Using manure for growing vegetables and other crops is nothing new. Agriculture took a step forward in the second half of the 1900s with the introduction of synthetic fertilizers and agrochemicals. Yields dramatically increased. Millions more were fed, albeit with many still going hungry. In recent times, there has been a surge of interest in organic produce in rich countries such as the UK. But claims that food grown in this old-fashioned way is "better for us" have not been supported by research. Food produced by conventional modern farming is safe and equally nutritious. Furthermore, the lower yields of organic farming cannot hope to deliver anywhere near enough food for an expanding human population. And this last point is invariably avoided.

Organic fertilizers are, indeed, natural. They come from decaying matter that was once alive. But the inorganic fertilizers of conventional farming are equally as natural; they are merely chemical, rather than bio-chemical. And where have they come from? Planet Earth, of course - not from the Prince of Darkness's bum.

A general ignorance of science, combined with a shortage of clear thinking, is exploited by the advertising industry. They commonly use the term "natural" to sell us all kinds of things. This word has wonderful connotations of a healthy lifestyle, free from the stress of modern city living. Many of us apparently feel uplifted by the idea, so we are quick to bite when presented with the bait. And I am a huge fan of the natural world, working hard to preserve and restore it. But the idea that "natural" is always good for you is an over-simplified myth. Watching a pride of lions from the safety of your safari vehicle is to be encouraged, but getting out of the vehicle and

> *"There are, in fact, two things: science and opinion. The former begets knowledge, the latter ignorance."*
>
> Hippocrates

walking up to the lions wouldn't be advisable. You might be naturally killed and eaten. Poisonous snakes are likewise part of the natural world, but can be deadly. Many plants are toxic and pose a serious risk of illness, injury, or death. Some plants are toxic unless artificially processed (think cooking) before consumption, common examples being the raw potato and uncooked red kidney beans. So it's best to think more precisely.

As a final example of myth vs. reality, there was the "curse of the cover" at the 2011 IAAF World Championships in Deagu, South Korea. Day after day, athletes who featured on the cover of the daily programme failed to win. Usain Bolt shockingly false started in the 100m final and was disqualified. Yelena Isinbayeva, the brilliant Russian pole vault champion with an astonishing 27 world records behind her, finished sixth. Only one athlete who featured on the cover in the first seven days managed to win and that was Olga Kaniskina in the 20km walk - the only event on what was otherwise a rest day.

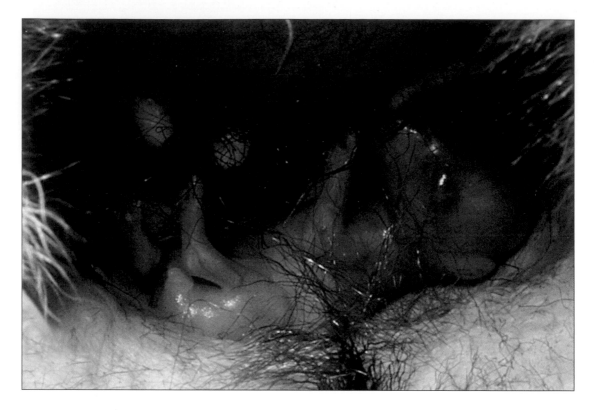

*Above and far right:*
*Australian wallabies*
*are renowned jumpers.*
*The species featured is*
*the common red-necked*
*wallaby. The image*
*above was one of the*
*more demanding I have*
*ever attempted to take.*

Australian Sally Pearson was selected for the cover on Day 8. She stormed her 100m hurdles semi-final with a personal best time that was the fifth best time ever. In the final, 90 minutes later, she ran 12.28 seconds to easily win gold - the fourth fastest time of all time and another personal best. Interviewed after the race, as she signed the cover of a programme, Sally Pearson said "Stuff the bloody curse. I've worked too hard to let any bloody curse stop me from winning." For that alone, Saturday September 3rd 2011 was a good day.

## iii. Materialism delivers

There has never been so much choice. Holiday destinations are worldwide. Television sets are high definition, no longer restricted to the same old three or four channels. Designer clothing is on the high street and not just for the super rich. Cars are slicker. Why not treat

yourself to a new kitchen? Or have a face lift or boob job? Smart phones get smarter. Food choices get more exotic. And a Beyoncé concert in 2011 offers more high-octane glitz than Lulu did in the '60s.

Materialism reliably delivers. You just need to keep splashing the cash. It all has a price. Spoilt for choice, numerous opportunities exist for self-expression, entertainment, and "I want". There is more than enough to distract and to be distracted. And that is another hurdle.

This proliferation of materialism has led to an overall lowering of values. Money talks and has become the new god. Owning the right fashionable possessions is more commonly judged to be desirable than having qualities such as integrity or truthfulness. Standards of discipline and self-discipline have declined. Mediocrity and dumbing down are applauded.

Widespread availability of this-that-and-the-other makes it easier to suppress any problems. Perhaps you run to the fridge to comfort eat, buy a new dress or pair of shoes, change your hairstyle, or snort a line or two of cocaine. And there's always booze to help drown your sorrows. That stylish exterior merely hides inner turmoil or poverty. If materialism makes it easier to be distracted in the short-term, you effectively forget the gap left by a lack of deeper meaning or purpose. Before you know it, many years have rolled by and you've sold out.

To be clear, I am not anti-materialistic and I am certainly in favour of technological development. Television, after all, played a crucial part in me going off to Ethiopia. What I am describing above is how excessive materialism is being pushed on everyone and linked with ambition. I would argue that our aspirations should be higher if life for all is to improve.

## iv. "Be just and fear not"

I am a Carlisle United supporter and our motto is "Be just and fear not" (originally from Shakespeare). I considered it as a possible title for this book. Being true to yourself and your principles is a basic requirement for developing better psychological health. But a motto is only a motto and most seem to ignore Shakespeare's good advice. "Be bland and

> *"Everyone's wearing a disguise to hide what they've got left behind their eyes."*
>
> Abandoned Love
> Bob Dylan

fit in" would seem the modern replacement - although many of the bland would dispute being labelled as dull as dishwater.

Pay-for-it materialism provides plenty of opportunity for having fun, as we have seen. Differing degrees or expressions of stroppiness seem to otherwise define many people's individuality, ranging from easy going to high maintenance. Ethical convictions are nowadays somewhat forgotten - or weakened by the above, if/when they are held. Most people seem far away from demonstrating any stand-up-and-be-counted characteristics.

Perhaps you then decide something is missing. And here comes yet another hurdle. Yes, you begin to look for that "something more". But you are also handicapped by the years of habit of too easily fitting in, lacking prior experience of really being true to yourself. Mixed with the mess of various emotions is the one which probably has the most debilitating power: fear. This can stop logical thinking. It is a wall that you seemingly cannot go beyond. Fear is a show stopper

Fear is produced by previous instances of disappointment, loss, or rejection. Whether you realise it or not - be it obvious or subtle - fear has got you by the short and curlies. The consequences of giving in to fear are simply expressed: you become less. Defensiveness restricts you. The play-it-safe limitations turn you into someone second-class, third-class, or worse. Everyone is at the mercy of fear, but there are different leagues or divisions, with promotion or relegation possible in the on-going drama of life. You may eventually realise that you have become comfortably numb. As the years go by, you accept this stuckness, seeing others around you likewise semi-paralysed. At least there is companionship and safety in numbers. But you have become a zombie in zombieland, part of the living dead, bitten or otherwise infected.

Emerging from this mass hypnosis requires sustained courage, as well as a clear understanding of the overall situation. Such emergence must not be confused with some minimal effort, possibly resulting in nothing more than a change of league or division. Shakespeare's wise advice is "Be just and fear not", not "Be just and fear less." You must learn to push through, even when that wall of fear is trying to stop you. Initially, this will probably mean living with the uncomfortable

*"Please lay down your thoughts of being no one. Concentrate on what you ought to be."*

*For No One*
Barclay James Harvest

*"Everyone's a no one 'til he wants to make a stand."*

*For No One*
Barclay James Harvest

*Above: Vicky and Wussy with a delivery of fencing wire. Vicky (left) is fond of saying "You need balls to do this work!"*
*So I gave them each a "balls" scarf as a present. (Each roll of wire, by the way, weighs 50kg.)*

*Far right: Are you willing to stand up and be yourself? (Spiloxene capensis at The Tortoise Farm.)*

feelings of vulnerability and apprehension. Eventually, you realise that the only thing to fear is fear itself.

As the vast majority continue to choose monotony, you have to be willing to do what you think is best. At the beginning, this may have the effect of rocking the proverbial boat, as some may persuade you to sit down again. If this happens, ask yourself if you are happy to carry on drifting. Remember that there is a greater life on the distant shore. As they say in tennis, keep your eye on the ball.

Be willing to stand alone if necessary. Being a pioneer has always required the strength to stand on your own two feet and not back down. It is crucial to hold your ground and not turn around, even when others are calling you back to the drifting boat going nowhere. Don't be dragged down any longer. Be true to what you think is right. There isn't an "easy" way forward.

# 6

# Going beyond

## i. Fitful dreams

The "flower power" era of the late 1960s and early 1970s was a false dawn. This counter-culture movement began in America as a reaction to the Vietnam War. Protesters offered flowers to the military police as a symbolic gesture. Rock music was new, young people were experimenting with psychedelic drugs, and the birth control pill allowed a more open attitude to sexual expression. "Love and peace" became the rallying call for a generation that was anti-establishment.

One of many student demonstrations against the war took place on May 4th 1970 at Kent State University, Ohio. It ended tragically when the National Guard fired into the crowd for 13 seconds. Neil Young's song *Ohio* - recorded by Crosby, Stills, Nash, and Young soon afterwards - summed it up: "Four dead in Ohio" and "What if you knew her and found her dead on the ground?" The song became an anthem to those who wanted to stand up and be counted, with the words "We're finally on our own" inspiring many. Another Crosby, Stills, Nash, and Young classic, *Find the Cost of Freedom*, echoed the same theme.

*Right and far right:* The saying "Can a leopard change its spots?" challenges whether transformation is possible.

*"I want to know
what became
of the changes
we waited for
love to bring.
Were they only
the fitful dreams
of some greater
awakening?"*

*The Pretender*
Jackson Browne

*"We thought
we could change
this world
with words like
love and freedom."*

*The Sad Cafe*
The Eagles

The band Chicago featured an audio clip of a previous demonstration that took place on August 29th 1968 on their first album released in April 1969, with the protesters repeatedly chanting "The whole world is watching." These defiant words continue again and again as the next track *Someday* begins, again echoing the need for change. In the UK, The Who recorded *Won't Get Fooled Again* and The Beatles joined the hippie movement with *All You Need is Love*.

By the mid to late '70s, punk rock had taken over. Johnny Rotten provoked an audience with "Bet you don't hate us as much as we hate you!" *God Save the Queen* lyrics included "She ain't no human being" and claimed that England had "no future". Revelling in raw anger and confusion had replaced the earlier aim of love, peace, and understanding.

Some travelled to India in search of enlightenment. Others started communes as a "way forward", in the spirit of togetherness. But the travellers got diarrhoea and the communes quickly crumbled. And the "me, me, me" mentality remained.

## ii.  Is change possible?

I have found no reliable evidence (outside the partial success of our own work) that non-selfishness can be taught. Seekers keep on seeking. Teachers keep on teaching. Preachers keep on preaching. Confusion and delusion persist. And some, understandably, give up the search.

Academics are convinced that higher consciousness states do occur - that is, those who can be bothered to examine this tricky subject. But the million dollar question remains: Can you really teach the ineffable? Going back at least three or four thousand years, there is knowledge available that seems relevant. But is it complete? Or reliable? There is certainly a long history of failure in being able to successfully teach or learn this better way, simply proven because selfishness continues. Phone technology rapidly advances, based on precise knowledge, but spirituality still relies on hope and faith.

Did I fail with the old team? Yes, in one way I did. They partially changed, but real progress was limited. Almost all failed to reach my

stated aim of an 80% shift. Despite this, I remain absolutely sure that non-selfishness can be taught and learned. It is just a matter of precise education.

*Above: The first light of dawn, well before sunrise, at Monument Valley, Utah, USA.*

Way back in 1980, my friend Marc was learning how to drive. One day, he crashed a Ford Transit into five parked cars and demolished a garden wall. He was upset at the chaos he had caused and so quit the lessons. But was he incapable of driving? Or was this just a case of insufficient learning? We all know that the driving of cars, vans, buses, and lorries is achievable - and so did Marc, who eventually re-started his lessons some time later and passed his test.

In *Actions Speak Louder Than Words*, I outlined what I have called the "Roger Bannister effect". The experts all said that no human being would ever run a mile in under four minutes. Then, on May 6th 1954, Roger Bannister did the "impossible". John Landy, an Australian, had previously failed in a number of serious attempts; he doubted anyone would run faster in the next ten years. Yet just 46 days after Bannister's

*Above:* *Becky looking for Cape mountain zebra at Komsberg.*

famous success, John Landy ran quicker to set a new world record. Several dozen other runners also ran quicker than four minutes in the first year after Roger Bannister had demonstrated it was achievable. Many more did so the following year and the world record was quickly broken again and again. The perception of what is "impossible" and "achievable" was pivotal. After Roger Bannister's breakthrough, the floodgates opened.

Others have never really considered me to be an example of learning how to change. I was already "the Enlightened One" when they met me. Numerous oneness experiences had led up to this final change - and they knew this, even though I repeatedly said that such ecstatic glimpses are unnecessary for anyone following a systematic educational path. I am not "special" and I shit and wee like everybody else. I have done my best to show my down-to-earthness.

Thankfully, Becky proved to be the exception when she began to profoundly change. Jonathan - who is always cautious and measured

in his responses - said that the words "dramatic" and "drastic" didn't go far enough to describe the shift. Sarah was astounded and intrigued, immediately asking lots of probing questions. Other members of the team seemed lost for words. At last, we now had an in-progress example of significant change.

*Above: A small group of Cape mountain zebra on one of Komsberg's steep mountainsides. This species almost became extinct, with only 91 individual animals surviving in 1950.*

## iii. Becky

No one expected that Becky would be different. She had been part of the team for three years and didn't stand out as being exceptional. So what happened? Becky explains in her own words:

*"The change was triggered when I started falling in love with Iain. For the first time, in any area of my life, I didn't give myself the option of failing. I massively raised my self-expectations and threw myself in, totally determined to make it work. It was time to 'risk' letting go of*

83

***Above:*** *Becky at Proposal Point.*

all the things with which I had fooled myself. I knew, with no doubt whatsoever, that I could succeed.

"Falling in love is an obvious time in people's lives when they open up and let down barriers. One of the reasons why this is not maintained, let alone built upon, is that it is largely about what they can get from the relationship. In this relationship, I understood that I wanted to really give. For me, supporting and sharing my life with someone who was so incredible was beyond all my dreams.

"I started looking into many areas of my life that were shoddy and unacceptable. My level of mental activity and alertness was still too dull. This was one of the first things that changed. I began seriously using what Iain has described as 'seeing' which brought about a pheno-menal change in clarity and personal responsibility. I worked out what was important and necessary, and threw out most of the thoughts and actions that were irrelevant to making a difference. Virtually all confu-sion went and I felt 'plugged in'.

*"As a result of thinking so much more, my feeling started to flow. For the first time, I cared properly and felt responsibility for people and life. I also quickly built up the ability to be off myself, the vast majority of the time.*

*"One area was particularly difficult. My strongest defence mechanism was to lie or bullshit. Facing reality in this area was more challenging than any other. Seeing the consequences of my behaviour, and facing the fact that people saw through me, plus wanting to learn, finally got me to change. I am now an ex-liar.*

*"Getting together with Iain was only a trigger and should not be confused as anything more. I had built up enough understanding over the three years prior to this to enable me to quickly put a number of pieces together and act on them.*

*"In conclusion, I went to a completely different level of seriousness to enable me to change. This seriousness continued to build for the next few months as I saw through the different layers of selfishness which had kept me stuck for so many years. Although only getting to about 90% of the way there, I have freed myself up. I have chosen not to oppress myself. I know who I am and what I still need to work on, and I can tackle most things with a reasonable chance of success. Nearly all small-mindedness has gone and I have become balanced and capable. My life is not about me and my limiting self-image; it is about being a tool and using my time to make a difference. I don't easily recognise who I was before this time."*

Becky's surge forward happened in 2003 and she has since played a crucial role in our work. She is understated, yet inspirational to all those who know her. Becky is making a difference. And she proposed to me at Komsberg on Valentine's Day, 2004, at a place now known as Proposal Point. Surprised but happy, I quickly said "yes".

## iv. Re-building the team

Most of the old team were already too accepting of their self-imposed ceilings by the time of Becky's transformation. Her example was undeniable but came too late, as it didn't penetrate their complacency. As I explained earlier, we needed to re-build the team.

*"Bound, I am bound, like the knots in a string eager to be where my life can begin. Out of the shadow and into the sun, so many things that I should have done. I will untangle myself so that I can see. I will untangle myself everything will be loving and free."*

*Loving and Free*
Kiki Dee

Nothing new was required. That said, our selection process to find suitable team members has become more rigorous and our interview process now extends to a three-month trial period. Candidates are still average, but we look for individuals with the spirit of an adventurer and sufficient intelligence to understand the concepts of change. Those who have excessive emotional issues which cloud the ability to think clearly are deemed unsuitable.

It has been a bit of a struggle to find appropriate people, compared to years ago. Society has changed. The lure of materialism, combined with less self-discipline and a lowering of ethical values, is a major factor. The trend is to blame and bitch, rather than respect and calmly consider. Whereas many were interested when I first spoke out, the focus today is more centred on fun and fantasy. Surveys of young people in the 1960s placed financial and material gain well down the list of aspirations. Ambitions have now reversed, with the accumulation of wealth being highly rated. Thankfully, however, some people still want to change the world.

*Above:* Becky and Wussy in our storage barn at Komsberg with a pile of wooden straining posts.

*Far left:* Becky and Happy, an orphaned baby black-backed jackal that we had to hand-rear at Komsberg beginning in October 2011.

*Avoidance Doesn't Work*

***Above***: *Vicky and Wussy on the fence line putting up droppers. We have erected 98km or 61 miles of boundary fencing.*

We have slightly adjusted our emphasis in a few key areas. We now really stress the need for continual improvement, warning of future complacency. And we go on and on about the importance of personal responsibility within the group. Our training to promote self-honesty has also been tweaked upwards, as we do our best to encourage an attitude of "avoid nothing".

Becky's example and watchful eye is a welcome addition to my own contribution. Her level of significant change has set the bar of achievability higher from the start. If she can do it, why not others? (The same argument has always been true of myself, of course, but my previous explanation of the need for an in-progress role model still stands.)

Vicky and Wussy have both been outstanding in their unstinting loyalty, support, and duty during this re-building stage. Their work at Komsberg and The Tortoise Farm has not just kept us on track but also allowed us to move forward at a time of fewer team members.

Their own levels of taking responsibility have accordingly increased. Several photographs of them in this book hopefully reflect their crucial input.

It is still far too early to say with confidence that we will succeed. But we should. The initial signs are looking very promising. The new team spirit and recent recruits are showing that our adjustments are working. Individual determination to push the boundaries, inwardly as well as outwardly, is sharper than before. There is a healthy intolerance to complacency within the team. We do, however, still need other would-be pioneers to join us. Meanwhile, our wildlife work is going from strength to strength. This is an exciting time.

*Above: Walking to work at Komsberg, old and new team members together. Rachel (far left) commented "The dedication and determination of the team needed at Komsberg is inspirational and matches the huge wilderness. I am not prepared to do less than my best."*

# 7

# Fiasco

## i. Question

Previously, in Chapter 3, I described the gross ineffectiveness and inefficiency of humanitarian aid organisations. Similar problems are found within the environmental and conservation areas. In my fifth book, *Holding On*, I asked what must be a relevant question: Why are tigers and rhinos still endangered after 50 years of conservation effort? I am shamelessly going to repeat some of what I have written about this in *Holding On*, as it serves as another useful and relevant example of self-interest and psychological avoidance in a situation where it might be least expected.

For every 100 rhinos living in the early 1970s, only three remained by the turn of the century - a terrible decline of 97%. The tiger's plight is just as bad or possibly worse. These are well-known megafauna. Huge amounts of money have been donated to this worthwhile cause, year after year, decade after decade. So what has it been used for? What's gone wrong?

I am going to mainly focus on the non-government organisations (NGOs), usually known as charities by the public in the UK. But, first, I need to briefly say something about other conservationists. It is easy

*Right and far right:*
*Tigers and rhinos are still endangered after 50 years of conservation effort.*

to criticise governments and, as we all know, this is often justified. They can and should do better. Many suffer from blatant corruption and apathy. However, the national parks system in many countries must be praised, as well as the many smaller reserves run by regional government authorities. Tanzania, Kenya, South Africa, and the USA are good examples of this. Governments have set aside quite a lot of land for nature, albeit not yet enough, and it is important to give credit where it is deserved.

Business people are also making a difference. South Africa is the most obvious example of a country where rich individuals and companies have started their own private nature reserves. Farmers, too, sometimes convert some or all of their land to benefit wild animals. Indeed, it was a few conservation-minded farmers who saved the black wildebeest in South Africa from going extinct in the late 1800s.

Academic researchers are often, quite frankly, just academic researchers. Most do little that is practically constructive, preoccupied with the survival of their own careers as they chase the next grant. With occasional exceptions, I think of them as "shiny bums". Knowledge is important but we are already highly knowledgeable. What we need now is the wisdom to apply our existing knowledge to situations that urgently need to be changed, not more research of dubious benefit. Many researchers stay cocooned within universities and other academic institutions. And they collectively use up a lot of funding available for conservation that could surely be better used.

## ii. Pointers

The NGOs pride themselves on having a special status that is relatively free from government bureaucracy and political pressure. This is supposed to encourage innovation and the freedom to act appropriately and quickly. NGOs like to think they can show governments a thing or two and believe they are ethically ahead of businesses. These organisations have worthwhile aims which the public support, usually believing they are "the good guys". This is the theory.

Sadly, the reality often falls well short of the promise or claims. Unlike governments, NGOs are relatively unaccountable. The general

> *"The significant problems we face cannot be solved at the same level of thinking we were at when we created them."*
>
> Albert Einstein

92

public continue to support them with regular donations regardless of success or failure. After all, "They care!" If, for example, there is a new surge of tiger or rhino poaching, the NGOs launch a fresh appeal for funds and the money comes pouring in. How many letters or emails are written by past or present donors questioning what has happened to the huge amount of money already given? How many people have even asked the question "Why are tigers and rhinos still endangered after 50 years of conservation effort?" Would businesses still be in business if they likewise failed to deliver in such a spectacular way?!

The makers of a British television documentary made an excellent point when they set up a spoof charity for the day, calling themselves "Daylight Robbery". Members of the public generously put money into their collecting tins, seemingly not bothering to think or question. The following response didn't arouse suspicion either: "Thank you. We'll use your money to help our mates escape from prison!" Indeed, some people gave money a second time when these words were said

*Above:* *Black wildebeest at Komsberg. In the late 1800s, only 550 survived.*

- and even congratulated the spoof Daylight Robbery fundraisers when they then added "That will help us buy a ladder or rope to get them over the walls!"

Let's look in more detail at the NGOs, starting off with how the donors' money is actually spent. Most staff in the majority of charity organisations nowadays get paid. And they pay themselves a higher wage than many imagine. Do your own investigations to find out how much a typical charity director is paid each year and how much the total staff budget adds up to; you will probably be surprised. Add to this all the office and administration costs, plus miscellaneous expense accounts. And the questionable fundraising costs, including the hiring of separate businesses that of course take their share. I hope you're starting to get the idea.

After this come the actual project expenses. But what do the charities really do? How do they specifically go about saving the endangered tiger and rhinos? Education is part of any solution and, conveniently, this often uses up a lot of the budget. But, in the UK, aren't we already sufficiently aware of the problems? Shouldn't these charities be putting most of their educational efforts towards changing the mindset of people living elsewhere in the world, specifically those who use the tiger parts and rhino horns? Or is this just too difficult, compared to sitting in a comfortable head office in Surrey or elsewhere? How many British conservationists actually work in Yemen, for example, where we know that a lot of poached rhino horn is used to make handles for ornamental daggers - a place where Arabic is the language with many ancient dialects and fewer people speaking any English than in most Arab countries? Isn't it crucially important to focus attention where it is most needed?

We all know about these wild animals being poached and of the need for anti-poaching squads. However, you would be surprised by how many times I have seen the on-the-ground reality where the anti-poaching staff are blatantly ill-equipped. They lack bullets for their rifles. Their communication equipment is non-existent or doesn't work. They don't even have basic repair kits for their bicycles or enough fuel or spare parts for their vehicles. And yet the staff at head office always seem to have the latest computers and plenty of money

*Far left: A white rhino with a good horn.*

***Above:*** *White rhino at rest, with oxpeckers.*

to attend the next international conference to talk still more about the problems.

I am not saying that these conservationists don't care, because they do, at least to some degree (albeit buried beneath a pile of excuses). However, I am certainly questioning their effectiveness and efficiency - their basic ability to correctly prioritise what most needs to be done and then to put these top concerns into action. Are these self-appointed conservationists actually doing what is really necessary? Or are they just conveniently choosing what to do and what not to do according to their own personal limitations? Is all the clever-sounding jargon about "grants" and "conservation partners" merely a smoke screen for doing less than their best, whilst getting reasonably well paid and being able to fool themselves that they're doing something useful? Wouldn't any salesman or manager in a business have been sacked long ago if there had been a 97% fall in profits?

## iii. Honest admission

After decades of abysmal decline, numbers of white rhino and black rhino started to slightly increase over a few short years up to 2007. This was effectively due to the good work by government-run places such as Kruger National Park in South Africa and Etosha National Park in Namibia, together with a number of private nature reserves in South Africa. Indeed, South Africa conserves 93% of all southern white rhino. These animals have a high monetary value and any surplus rhinos are sold to private nature reserves, with the owners willing to invest. But because the demand for rhino horn remains high - after 50 years of alleged education and other efforts by NGOs - this minor upturn is being undone. South Africa began seeing a rise in poaching during 2008, with at least 83 rhinos killed. It got worse in 2009 when 122 rhinos were poached. And in 2010, the situation became shocking with 333 rhinos killed by organised gangs - including 146 lost from the Kruger

*Above:* *Black rhino at a waterhole, late afternoon.*

*Above:* Anti-poaching guards on duty at Kruger National Park.

population. A further 448 rhinos have been slaughtered in 2011. And these figures are from just one country, which has the best track record of all for breeding rhino in the wild during recent times.

In October 2011, WWF and the International Rhino Foundation announced the extinction of the Javan rhino sub-species in Vietnam, leaving less than 44 surviving Javan rhinos in Indonesia's Ujung Kulon National Park. No resignations or dismissals were announced.

A month later, the International Union for Conservation of Nature (IUCN) declared the West African sub-species of the black rhino extinct. They also announced that a sub-species of the white rhino in central Africa was now possibly extinct. The IUCN's 2011 annual update listed more threatened species of wildlife than ever before.

Alarm bells sounded in the 1960s about the tiger facing extinction, with several crisis warnings since. In 2000, the United Nations Convention on Trade in Endangered Species published a report saying that tiger poaching was accelerating and that officials and conservation

*Above: A tiger emerges into this beautiful forest clearing.*

groups were refusing to face up to the problem. The report concluded that "an essential first step in solving any problem is to face up to its existence." I am not a fan of the various UN organisations, as they talk the talk at considerable expense, but it is worth repeating their shocking words yet again: "an essential first step in solving any problem is to face up to its existence." These words were written after 40 years of international conservation effort to help save the tiger. They went on to criticise WWF's office in India which "has apparently been so absorbed in recent years with its own problems that it has failed to motivate stronger action from public authorities." I know this to be true because I have seen it for myself, in the years before 2000 and since.

By the beginning of 2005, the tiger crisis became a farce when it was obvious that all of the tigers had disappeared from Sariska National Park in Rajasthan, India. For several months ridiculous excuses were made, such as "the tigers are hiding" and "they have migrated but will

*Above: Looking up. What is the tiger's future?*

come back". The denial, by those who should have known better, was at its most blatant.

Under pressure, the Prime Minister of India eventually acted and sent in the Central Bureau of Investigation (CBI) to find out what had happened at Sariska. Despite lacking previous wildlife experience, the CBI rapidly investigated and produced an excellent report. In stark contrast to some NGOs, their conclusions were blunt and accurate.

Fateh Singh Rathore died on 1st March 2011, aged 72. Many years before, under the no-nonsense political leadership of Indira Gandhi, Fateh Singh took charge of the Ranthambhore tiger reserve in Rajasthan. In 1976, he successfully negotiated the resettlement of 13 villages containing some 10,000 families from inside Ranthambhore to a new village outside. He inspired dedication amongst many forest guards and urged them to perform their duty well. The tigers subsequently flourished, seen by countless tourists from all over India and from many countries throughout the world.

Fateh Singh's efforts were not popular with everyone. In 1981 he was ambushed, beaten unconscious, and left for dead by villagers who were illegally cutting wood and grazing cattle in the reserve. By 1988, he had been sacked as warden of Ranthambhore and transferred to a desk job in Jaipur after challenging a rich and influential man caught shooting wild boar.

When I met Fateh Singh Rathore shortly after this time, he never claimed to have been an angel - but he was obviously and genuinely intent on saving the tiger from the ravages of over a billion people in his country. In typical flamboyant style, Fateh Singh bluntly told me that "99.999% of my people are liars and cheats"; he briefly paused, adding "and they should be six foot under." During the early years, at various conferences, Fateh Singh warned the international conservation organisations against complacency, saying that the tiger was far from safe. In those days, Project Tiger was considered to be the flagship of the conservation movement - a rare success story. Valmik Thapar, who worked closely with Fateh Singh regarding him as his mentor, honestly admitted to me that even he had wondered if Fateh was going too far during those times - until later, when the predicted cracks started to appear.

Valmik Thapar has done much more than most to try to save the tiger in India. He has written a number of books, informed the public about tigers through presenting wildlife documentaries, and he has used his position to influence policy makers up to the highest level. Furthermore, he co-founded an NGO working with villagers around Ranthambhore to help alleviate their poverty and in doing so win support for the tiger and its natural forest. And, in his own words, he has failed.

Valmik says so himself:

> "I established the Ranthambhore Foundation in 1988 to try and find peace and harmony amongst people, tigers, and the forests. I was idealistic and believed there was a way. In the 1990s, Ranthambhore Foundation focused on various issues including dairy development, increasing milk yields, enhancing income generation of women through handicrafts and agro-forestry. But they all failed. All my work in

*"Honesty is the first chapter in the book of wisdom."*

Thomas Jefferson

> creating Ranthambhore Foundation and trying to do something to integrate man, nature, and tigers failed. The Ranthambhore Foundation is a failure. I gave it up in the [late] 1990s."

He continues:

> "I accept failure fully. I am the first one who shouts to all that I have failed in my life. My life's mission was to make sure that tigers could be saved. I believed I could do it. I met the Prime Minister, the present one, the last one, and the one before that, the leader of the opposition, and various MPs."

## iv. Problem

Where is a similar level of self-honesty from all the other individual conservationists, NGOs, and governments? It isn't anywhere to be seen. Self-honesty is like Monty Python's proverbial Norwegian blue parrot: it is no more, gone, expired; it has become deceased.

Today's average shallow-thinking environmentalist is lacking. Image has replaced the need to be truly capable. Saying the right words has been substituted for having authentic human values such as integrity and wisdom. Psychological avoidance is the norm, yet is ignored. There is safety in numbers if you don't rock the boat, neatly negating the need to "be just and fear not". So, not surprisingly, endangered wild animals such as the tiger and rhinos remain in serious peril.

The fundamental problem yet again is the "me, me, me" mentality. The most blatant acts of selfishness are recognised as such, but the majority of this normalised self-orientated behaviour is almost universally accepted and so goes unchallenged. Multiply it by 7 billion people and wildlife has a serious problem. And what really happens when someone decides to care for nature? Bolting on a bit of caring for wild animals or adding good intentions to "me, me, me" doesn't actually change much - because the basic difficulty and existing psychological baggage still remain. This baggage seriously impacts on individual capability and project performance.

*"Insanity is continuing to do the same thing over and over and expecting different results."*

Albert Einstein

102

There is an obvious need for transparency with both NGOs and governments. But how will this actually happen when the individuals are full of psychological baggage, always ready to make the next excuse? Currently, project planning or evaluation doesn't even recognise this basic dysfunctional human factor - because it is so normalised. Add avoidance to the equation and ask why should anything change when the "do nothing" option of continued mutual bullshitting remains, merely allowing more of the same? Therefore, in the acceptable world of "I'm alright, Jack", the tigers and rhinos keep on being endangered - with yet another NGO conference taking place or newsletter due out tomorrow. "Would you please donate £3 every month to our worthwhile cause?"

*Above: I photographed this white rhino at Kruger on my 50th birthday. Has it since been poached?*

# 8

# Minefields

## i. Emotional mess

Becky and I were in Eastbourne public library, waiting to take out a book on loan. In front of us was a mother with her young son. The boy, possibly five years of age, wanted to hire a film on DVD. His mother, seemingly respectable and in her thirties, replied that he already had it at home in his DVD collection. The youngster insisted "But I want it!" and the mother promptly gave in. The attending female librarian, in her early twenties, was excellent and responded with "Be a good mummy and do exactly what you're told!" I found out that she had recently become a mother herself and was appalled at this all-too-common example of bad parenting.

Normal consciousness is an emotional mess. As this dysfunction is normalised, it is therefore underestimated or too readily accepted. It is not only those at the extremes who are sick. Everyone is mixed up, perpetuated by social conditioning. Contradictions frequently go unchecked. Avoidance does what it says on the proverbial tin.

Emotional dysfunction can be outwardly displayed in blatantly obvious behaviour or it can be more subtle, even hidden from view. Multiple variations of flawed conduct can be found throughout this

**Right:** *An Eritrean refugee at Awad el Sid, Sudan. Who cares?*

**Far right:** *Have you spotted the second yellow-footed rock-wallaby?*

104

entire spectrum, but they all boil down to maladjustment to some degree or another. And avoidance is the underlying factor.

Perhaps you then begin to search for something deeper in your life, developing an interest in higher concerns. But this is likely to merely distract or disjoin you from what has gone before. You have already accumulated more emotional baggage than you care to admit. And this effectively presents you with a minefield that will threaten your new journey of discovery. If you enter the minefield, probably unaware of what lurks beneath the surface, a series of explosions become inevitable. You are unprepared, untrained in detection and bomb disposal skills. Most just change course to steer clear of such disruption or perceived danger - and, in doing so, the way forward is lost. The journey has been corrupted.

## ii.  Brain

*"Do not call for black power or green power. Call for brain power."*

Barbara Jordan

The human brain was not designed. It evolved. And this simple fact provides a physiological explanation for the problem. Neuroscience is still working out how our brains function. However, we already know enough to make a couple of basic statements that should help us appreciate the situation and add to our understanding that education is vital. Before continuing, I would like to make clear that this is a complex and detailed subject. Myths and misunderstandings about how we use our brains are widespread. I do not want to add to such nonsense, yet I need to provide a simple summary using only a few words.

*"The brain is like a muscle. When it is in use we feel very good."*

Carl Sagan

An older part of our brain, in evolutionary terms, is commonly called the limbic system and is located below the cerebral cortex. It consists of a number of structures including the hippocampus that helps with the formation of long-term memories and the amygdala which produces the emotions of fear and anxiety. These gave us an evolutionary advantage in the early days of human existence when self-preservation, finding food, and outwitting dangerous animals was the name of the game. The limbic system is commonly called the "emotional brain" because it is important in producing emotional mood and emotional responses. When in South Africa at Komsberg or The Tortoise Farm, for example, I feel a sense of anxiety whenever I approach certain spots where I once had a scary encounter with a Cape cobra.

Rationally, I know that such a pre-programmed response is intended as a simple warning. The snake I previously happened upon is now probably elsewhere and might have since been eaten by an eagle or other predator. Such rational thoughts come from the frontal lobes in my brain and these help control the primative emotions of the limbic system. The frontal lobes are like an empty book in which we can write whatever we choose, according to what we are learning. They are a more recent evolutionary development or addition.

So the first statement we can safely make is to be aware that the human brain was not designed for use in the modern world. It has developed or evolved, but there can be contradictory signals if we do not understand what is what. We therefore need to master the use of our brains through taking personal control of ourselves and deciding upon the best course of action, rather than merely knee-jerk reacting. Yes, we must feel. But clear thinking is also essential if we are to live a life that goes way beyond the basics necessary for survival.

Our brains develop sophisticated neural pathways, consisting of myelin-insulated neurons. These connect different parts of the brain. A primary purpose of education is to stimulate more neural pathways so that we can handle more traffic or information. Associating a particular song with a particular event, thought, or feeling is an example of how this works in practice. Those individuals who are serious about achieving a clear ambition use continual association between different aspects of what they do, thereby reinforcing their aim. They are effectively building a route in their brains to success. Research has also demonstrated that repeated practice is essential to deep learning and that it works by adding extra layers of myelin around the neurons. These additional, multiple layers of myelin enable better bandwidth and therefore greater performance.

We therefore become hard-wired, to use a popular phrase. But the concept of neural plasticity goes a step further. Individual connections within the brain are constantly being removed/weakened or recreated/

*"I get so nervous on stage I can't help but talk. I try. I try telling my brain: stop sending words to the mouth. But I get nervous and turn into my grandma. Behind the eyes it's pure fear. I find it difficult to believe I'm going to be able to deliver."*

Adele

strengthened, largely dependent upon how they are used. Neurons that fire together, wire together - to put it simply - and neurons that fire apart, wire apart. So here we have a second reliable statement. And it helps that we are beginning to know the physical mechanisms of consciousness. Research challenges any assumption that there is an "easy" way to change. It suggests the need for consistency, as well as repeated practice. The saying "Be careful what you wish for" seems like good advice.

## iii. Ugly head

An adult is stuck with the hurt child. Troubles from the past are still active. Avoidance may help maintain the illusion that all is well, but it isn't. An explosion is waiting to happen. When this occurs, it is like rearing your ugly head. The madman suddenly appears. Or perhaps it shows up as big head, driven by arrogance. It could, perhaps, be dumb head or zombie head. In some, it takes the appearance of child-ish head.

Ugly head will attempt to sabotage your best efforts at going beyond yourself. It is a combination of all your insecurities and unresolved emotional pain, together with the release of raw emotion from part of your brain that you have not mastered. Ugly head is trying to defend you against further distress or disenchantment. It is attempting to shut you down or stop you, to keep you safe from new attack. Even though the better part of you yearns for that "something more". Dr Jekyll has met Mr Hyde.

Alternatively, do you remember the classic movie *Jaws*? Can you hear the music? Just when you thought it was safe to get back in the water.....the shark appears and bites your leg off. This is the same as ugly head.

Most people are already keeping clear of the water. Someone then re-enters the sea of dreams. If there is any emotional splashing, this might attract the attention of the shark. Caught unaware through the "it won't happen to me" avoidance, the shark comes out of nowhere and suddenly attacks.

*"They say that anger is just love disappointed."*

Hole in the World
The Eagles

***Far left:*** *An elephant never forgets.*

109

*Drawings kindly done
by Tutte Newall.*

Until you have significantly re-wired your brain through education or re-education, properly understanding the situation of life, you are vulnerable to sabotage by ugly head or attack from the shark. This may also try to cripple you if there is some "no go" area that you have refused to look at and resolve, leaving you vulnerable to attack. If you let this emotional side of you win, you may lose your dreams. You could end up walking away from your highest ambition, having made the wrong decision based on fear, the self-doubt of insecurity, and false justification. The understanding of logic and ethical values is forgotten. You mess up.

Leading sports personalities and managers are increasingly appreciating how this phenomenon can impact on sporting achievement, especially when an Olympic gold medal is at stake. I watched British cycling in the run-up to the 2008 Olympic Games with interest, as I could tell they knew more than most. When our cyclists won more medals in Beijing than any other country had ever previously achieved, it was not down to luck. It was planned. They were ready. And the psychology of what produces success - and what threatens to obstruct it - was understood.

Eminem perhaps explains this the best, in the lyrics of his smash hit *Lose Yourself* from the *8 Mile* movie:

*Look, if you had one shot, or one opportunity
To seize everything you ever wanted, one moment,
Would you capture it? Or just let it slip?*

*His palms are sweaty, knees weak, arms are heavy
There's vomit on his sweater already, Mom's spaghetti
He's nervous, but on the surface he looks calm and ready to drop bombs.*

*But he keeps on forgetting what he wrote down
The whole crowd goes so loud
He opens his mouth but the words won't come out
He's choking. Everybody's joking now
The clock's run out. Time's up, over
Snap back to reality
Oh, there goes gravity.*

# iv. Avoidance

Sigmund Freud (1856-1939) was the first psychologist to appreciate the importance of avoidance in relationship to anxiety. Others have since further developed our knowledge. However, I believe that psychology still hasn't fully grasped how avoidance is behind so much of current human behaviour.

As I was changing, I mapped out for myself the significance of avoidance through watching everyone else around me and comparing these observations with my own consciousness. I quickly discovered that people were astonishingly vulnerable to avoidance. If a touchy topic was brought up and pursued, there would be a switch from being rational to irrational. Interest or concern would be replaced with unresponsiveness. "I can't, because" excuses were commonly evoked, including by those with greater intelligence or more capability than average. Avoidance of reality, to differing degrees, was the norm.

I have written extensively about the various forms of avoidance and how this frustrates good intentions to change. The third section of *Actions Speak Louder Than Words* specifically outlines this problem and I would direct the reader to take serious notice of those chapters if you are interested in personal/spiritual/psychological development or whatever you prefer to call it.

Avoidance produces a veil or fog that reduces what is seen of reality. It distorts. You do not see others or situations as they really exist. This condition of illusion is supported through excuses, complacency, deliberate forgetfulness, the superficial game playing of self-expression, and the short-term fix of "I want more".

The tricks of avoidance are varied. As we have already seen, the retreat into fantasy and myth is common. Intellectualisation of the subject is a similar version. Trivialising reduces or minimises what should really be of considerable importance. Denial or repression is the most extreme form of avoidance, a measure of final desperation. Projection or displacement, often through blaming others as a convenient scapegoat, is much more common and frequently used nowadays. Shaggy made avoidance famous with his *It Wasn't Me* song - taking it all to ridiculous lengths.

> *"Our deepest fear
> is not that
> we are inadequate.
> Our deepest fear
> is that we
> are powerful
> beyond measure."*
>
> Nelson Mandela

*Avoidance Doesn't Work*

*Above: Stand tall and be alert.*
*The saddle-billed stork is one of my favourite birds.*

*Far right: How will you leave your mark?*

Start observing yourself and others. You will increasingly notice the patterns of avoidance are everywhere, used by everyone, helping to maintain self-orientated behaviour. Excuses roll off the tongue as easily as water from a tap. They go unchallenged, nobody wanting to cause upset. Gossip, bitching, and incessant chatter trivialises life. People tweet and twitter as if they have a bird brain, with nothing apparently better to do, ignoring a greater capacity for responsibility. Convenient stupidity is accepted as if part of being intelligent. "Fake it 'til you make it" is advised by an army of wannabes. Others keep their heads down, lie low, and try not to be noticed. Perhaps they get excited by the rush of the Boxing Day sales? Dumbed down and comfortably numb. Different expressions of the same thing. Obsessive avoidance. My starting advice would be to step back, open your eyes, put one and one together to make two, and don't be fooled any longer. Oh, yes, and be willing to be outcast for a while.

112

# 9
# Key issues

## i. Meaning and purpose

What is the meaning of life? Why are we here? These big questions have been asked over and over again. I think the answer is simple. We are intelligent beings, capable of working out what is happening in the world around us and within ourselves. Selfishness, even as a strategy for survival, is barely okay and only makes limited sense. It is problematic and causes much suffering. We know or sense this, even if avoidance dumbs us down with only a nagging doubt remaining.

As human intelligence increases, a better option becomes available. Non-selfishness - one for all and all for one - makes much more sense. And, ultimately, it eliminates most forms of suffering and therefore provides a greater freedom for individual expression and well-being. When there is sufficient intelligence to enable consideration and choice, the option of selfishness becomes crazy. Non-selfishness is obviously preferable. Avoidance threatens to frustrate progress. Ignorance of the minefields, including the peculiarities of our evolved brain, doesn't help. Precise knowledge and education are required.

Having explained what I understand meaning and purpose to be in the two paragraphs above as succinctly as possible, I now want to

*Right and far right:*
*We are presently*
*working hard to*
*re-introduce cheetah*
*to Komsberg.*

*"The purpose of life is not to be happy. It is to be useful, to be honorable, to be compassionate, to have it make some difference that you have lived and lived well."*

Ralph Waldo Emerson

provide three examples of what it is not. I am yet again risking the reader's annoyance, but - being a Carlisle United supporter, "Be just and fear not" - here goes as usual. Personal love and intimacy are very important, of course. But this is not enough. It does not constitute a deep meaning and purpose to life. The bigger issue of one for all and all for one remains - something which is even more important (or, at least, as important).

Family is also important, including the loving nurture of children. But, again, this is not a truly deep meaning and purpose. The Einstein quote in Chapter 4 has already suggested this, including the need to widen our circle of compassion to embrace all. As with personal love, it would be a mistake to confuse the support of family with the even bigger needs of the whole.

Thirdly, when I say one for all and all for one, I mean it. Therefore Christians must be wrong. The righteous believers will apparently go to heaven and the sinners to hell, eternally damned. Leaving aside my doubts about the possibility of an afterlife, heaven and hell or other-wise, I must go along with this belief for a moment or two. Personally, I would INSIST on going to hell. Even if I was offered entry into heaven because of all my "good work", I would have to respectfully refuse. It's not that I have anything against a bit of harp music - although I much prefer the acoustic or electric guitars, bass, keyboards, and drums of rock. It's just that there would be work still to do down below. As some people are seriously confused and far gone, it would take time to un-tangle the mess - but, hell, we'd have eternity. I wouldn't be content until the last person was fit for heaven - then I'd happily go through the gates, arm-in-arm with the final entrant, assuming I was offered a second pass. Anything less smells of small-mindedness to me and I'm surprised that Christians haven't dumped such a medieval divide-and-rule notion that doesn't do justice to their better teachings.

To conclude, any lesser interpretations of meaning and purpose are of limited value and actually insignificant when compared to what I am trying to convey. A vacuum is left when there is no purpose to life and it is understandable that there may be a wish to fill such an emptiness. Therefore, the search for meaningfulness can be - indeed, is frequently - dumbed down. There are still limited benefits, but these

*Far right*: *Cheetah on the Serengeti plains. Think more, care more, and do more.*

are proportional to the size of the bigger picture. The real depth has to include all. I trust I have sufficiently emphasised the words "deep" and "all".

## ii.  Values

Many people define themselves through their career and earnings, their house and car, their clothes and other possessions, their appearance, their husband or wife or partner, their children, and their popularity with others. A self-image is built up from these outward factors and additional ones.

Values offer a deeper approach to self-image. They provide a more solid and reliable foundation. Will today's style icons really be remembered in the future as we still respect those who stood tall in years gone by? Individuals such as Mahatma Gandhi, Winston Churchill, Martin Luther King, William "Braveheart" Wallace, Oskar Schindler, and Nelson Mandela are held in high esteem because they stood up for something that was worthwhile - something bigger and less transient than themselves.

Values come with a bigger price tag than an expensive handbag or car. The Dixie Chicks were a hugely popular country music band that rose to fame in the late '90s. They sold more CDs in 1998 than all other country music groups combined. Further commercial success followed, together with a string of awards and honours. Then, during a concert in London just ten days before the 2003 invasion of Iraq, lead vocalist Natalie Maines said "Just so you know, we're on the good side with y'all. We do not want this war, this violence. And we're ashamed that the President of the United States [George W. Bush] is from Texas." *The Guardian* newspaper quoted this in a review of the concert and the American media picked up on the story. What happened next in the Land of the Free shows what can happen when you dare to be brave.

A protest against the Dixie Chicks quickly gathered pace. Radio stations stopped playing their music. Dustbins were publicly positioned for former fans to throw away their Dixie Chicks CDs. Other demonstrations used tractors and bulldozers to crush the discarded albums. Remarks included "strap her to a bomb and drop her over Baghdad", "traitor", "Saddam's angels", "shut up and sing", "Dixie slut", and worse. A specific death threat was made for a concert in Dallas. Audiences halved, record sales plummeted, and sponsors dropped out. I personally remember watching the annual Country Music Awards on BBC2 late one night, surprised to see the Dixie Chicks being shunned. So many people were terrified to be associated with them.

They hit back in 2006 with the single *Not Ready To Make Nice*. By then, 59% of the American public thought the war in Iraq had been a mistake. Famously, no weapons of mass destruction had been found. The Dixie Chicks sang:

> *"I'm not ready to make nice*
> *I'm not ready to back down*
> *I'm still mad as hell and I don't have time*
> *To go round and round and round.*
> *It's too late to make it right*
> *I probably wouldn't if I could*
> *Cause I'm mad as hell*
> *Can't bring myself to do what it is you think I should."*

and

> *"I made my bed and I sleep like a baby*
> *With no regrets and I don't mind saying*
> *It's a sad sad story when a mother will teach her daughter*
> *That she ought to hate a perfect stranger.*
> *And how in the world can the words that I said*
> *Send somebody so over the edge*
> *That they'd write me a letter*
> *Saying that I better*
> *Shut up and sing or my life will be over."*

The song featured in every show of their Accidents & Accusations tour in 2006. But 14 concerts in the United States had to be cancelled due to poor ticket sales and others were delayed. The Dixie Chicks were warmly greeted elsewhere, including a concert back in London where Natalie announced "We've returned to the scene of the crime"

> *"Let's impeach*
> *the President*
> *for lying.*
> *And misleading*
> *our country*
> *into war."*
>
> *Let's Impeach the*
> *President*
> Neil Young

*Above:* The majestic gemsbok is one of several antelope species that we have re-introduced to Komsberg.

*Far right:* We have also released kudu to the lower valley section of Komsberg.

to tumultuous applause. In February 2007, they won five top Grammy awards including Song of the Year.

Ethical values are a measure of our awareness and integrity. They represent who and what we are. They define our behaviour, one way or another. If we are to be taken seriously by others, we should be serious about our values. The human race is still in its infancy or perhaps entering an adolescent stage, and so there is a need to grow up.

Ethical considerations are frequently ignored when "me, first" is strongly dominant. When there has been some moral development, values are then used if and as convenient. Therefore, people disagree about what is right and wrong - and contradictions can lead to intolerance, as the Dixie Chicks' example shows. Who will be brave? Who will stand up and be counted? It is easy to be a disruptive and confused rebel without a cause. It is even easier to conform and go along with the crowd. Being a person of integrity, with deeply held convictions and facing up to responsibility, requires a great deal more effort.

*Above:* *Too much choice can create confusion. Namaqualand flowers.*

### iii. Vision

Many years ago, I had two neighbours who were dissatisfied with their rat race lifestyle. They deliberately took time off work to go on holiday, so they could spend a few days thinking about their future. I was excited for them and therefore eager to find out what they had decided as soon as they returned. But when I knocked on their door, I was disappointed by their dull response. Sunshine and wine had apparently distracted them from their stated aim. They hadn't thought about anything and had seemingly forgotten why they even went.

Vision is important. It is the best you can imagine - a goal for the future. If values get you there and keep you there, then vision is the "there". The two v's go hand-in-hand.

Research suggests that too much choice creates confusion, often hindering or paralysing the ability to choose wisely. A story involving Sundous, the Sudanese director of our humanitarian aid work for

many years, is relevant here. Sundous was in England for talks about the future of the medical clinic. We were in a supermarket one day when she noticed a mother and child. They were at the biscuit shelves, picking up one packet after another and putting them back again, until finally making a selection. Sundous turned around to us, saying "This is why your people don't care about the suffering of my people."

If you are unsure of how to work out what you want - what you really, really want - start off by simplifying the options. What matters most of all? Once you've identified this, you can remind yourself that everything else matters less. Prioritise. Clearly and deliberately.

There is no "wrong time" - only excuses that will keep you stuck and numb. And you'll never be short of excuses if you want to keep making them. Tomorrow never comes. The idea of a "right time" is an idealistic myth. That knock on the door will probably never happen. Your future is up to you to make or break. Reliance on intuition is also a poor substitute for thoughtful decisiveness. Fear and other

*Above:* *The future is in your hands. Australia's endangered bridled nailtail wallaby.*

emotions are likely to be at work, making any choice vulnerable to limitations and therefore unreliable as a way forward.

Unless you are sub-normally messed up, first figure out a basic framework of values. Realise you have freedom of choice - to learn or not to learn, to change or remain the same. Be more willing to look at what you have previously avoided. Add whatever self-awareness you have got, of both strengths and weaknesses, to your framework of understanding. Then acknowledge it is best to progress and find some issue that motivates your involvement.

As your vision takes shape, make a plan. Organise your life to make time and space for turning your dream into a reality. In this busy materialistic world, you will probably have to prune back some of what distracts you. Extravagance and wastefulness may need to be replaced with a more thrifty approach. Less will enable more.

If you don't have a vision, you don't have direction. And remember that vision is best served with deep meaning and purpose. Without this, there is boredom and the cycle of "ups" and "downs". You will be more like a hamster on a wheel, going round and round, than a fully alive human being.

## iv.  Opportunity and hard work

In the early 1980s, in addition to establishing The Oasis, I seriously considered demonstrating my understanding of human potential by attempting to produce a world-class sports champion. Doing well at some sports is dependent upon having unusual physical attributes. If you don't have big lungs, for example, you can't realistically dream of being a top swimmer. And to play professional basketball, you have to be very tall. As many sports rely on youthfulness - and I only wanted to work with adults - the choice was further narrowed due to the need for a few years of training, beginning in someone's teens or younger. I eventually decided upon darts, perhaps enthralled by the battles that I watched on television between Eric Bristow, Jocky Wilson, and John Lowe (all forerunners of today's Phil Taylor). If anything, all you apparently needed to succeed in those days was a big beer belly.

*"Success is my only motherfucking option, failure's not."*

*Lose Yourself*
Eminem

124

Famine in Ethiopia decided the course of my action, in addition to our existing nature conservation commitments, leaving no free time. We'll never know if I could have produced a World Champion darts player, but I'm reasonably sure that I could have done so - or, at very least, a top ten player. Nevertheless, I later discovered that others were also understanding how to achieve outstanding success.

Laszlo Polgar is a Hungarian educational psychologist who came up with an even bolder plan than my own (at least, regarding the darts bit). He wanted to challenge the myth of talent and claimed that excellence could be learned. He was willing to experiment on his own children, as yet unborn. First, he needed a wife. Klara was an educator in Ukraine and, intrigued, she married Laszlo in 1967. They had three daughters. Polgar decided to teach them chess. All three have since achieved unquestionable acclaim in world chess, a game normally dominated by men. Susan, the eldest daughter, became the first woman in history to reach grandmaster status - one of many achievements. Sofia, the second born, also chalked up a series of remarkable successes in international chess. Judit, the baby of the family, became the youngest grandmaster of all time by the age of 15, when she beat the previous record held by Bobby Fischer. In addition to being the world's top female player, Judit has defeated almost all of the best male players including Garry Kasparov and Anatoly Karpov.

K. Anders Ericsson is a Swedish psychologist, now at Florida State University, specialising in the acquisition of expert performance and deliberate practice. Ericsson and others have been building evidence for what is commonly termed the 10,000 hours rule. This appears to be the amount of practice time needed to become a true expert - in anything. *Outliers* by Malcolm Gladwell (which I read in the spring of 2011) and *Talent is Overrated* by Geoff Colvin (which I haven't read) provide further details in popular format.

Evidence consistently and overwhelmingly shows that experts are made and not born. This has proved to be true in whatever fields of expertise that have been analysed. Having a "gift" would appear to be misleading. The words of Anders Ericsson - and his colleagues Michael Prietula and Edward Cokely - that I am about to quote could easily be mine, and they summarise the conclusions of this research:

*"It is not the mountain we conquer but ourselves."*

Edmund Hillary

*Above:*

*Comma in the wind.*
*It took this butterfly*
*more than 10,000 hours*
*to evolve into what it is.*

*"The journey to truly superior performance is neither for the faint of heart nor for the impatient. The development of genuine expertise requires struggle, sacrifice, and honest, often painful self-assessment. There are no shortcuts. It will take you at least a decade to achieve expertise, and you will need to invest that time wisely, by engaging in 'deliberate' practice - practice that focuses on tasks beyond your current level of competence and comfort. You will need a well-informed coach not only to guide you through deliberate practice but also to help you learn how to coach yourself."*

Thomas Edison, prolific inventor of the lightbulb and much more, famously said "Genius is 1% inspiration and 99% perspiration." Another Edison quote goes further: "Opportunity is missed by most people because it is dressed in overalls and looks like work." And again: "The first requisite for success is to develop the ability to focus and develop your mental and physical abilities to the problem at hand,

without growing weary. Because such thinking is often difficult, there seems to be no limit to which some people will go to avoid the effort and labour that is associated with it."

Please also re-read the Eminem lyrics quoted in Chapter 8 because they are equally relevant here. Choking, bottling it, or messing up is a common response to opportunity when fear – in whatever form rears its ugly head. You forget what you wrote down. The noise of the crowd grows so loud in your ears and head. Before you know it, you have fallen flat on your face and been counted out. Time's up and the chance to realise your dream is over. Disappointed, you snap back to the reality of life as a hamster on the treadmill going nowhere.

I identified four preliminary skills necessary for what I know as the way of *seeing* and *feeling* when I wrote *Human Potential - the search for that "something more"*. The first is a receptive alertness, the ability to be actively-passive or passively-active. The second is concentration. If you drift or wander in your mind, you cannot focus your attention.

*Above: Concentration is needed by this black-backed jackal for hunting.*

127

*Above:* *Conformity?*
*Or being yourself?*

I have already mentioned the third skill earlier in this book, namely the capacity for being true to yourself. And the fourth is simply to be able to act now. These four preliminary skills are essential for responding to opportunity, both initially and on a continual basis.

## v. Facing reality

Another young man is stabbed, leaving his family and friends devastated. A girl dreads going home, knowing her father is probably going to sexually abuse her yet again. A woman in her thirties goes to the doctor for more anti-depressant tablets; Prince Charming wasn't that good and her life sucks. A gang member looks to the gang for a sense of belonging, having received little or no love from his parents; he doesn't really want to hurt anyone, but nevertheless carries a knife "for protection" because it's what you do in his neighbourhood.

*Above: Overpopulation in the shape of 7 billion people is facing reality.*

Another possible title for this book was "Facing reality". This is vital if you want to get anywhere real. Acceptance of reality is a starting point en route to changing it. Bullshit won't help. Hope - where there is no actual basis for such optimism - will merely delude you, until life one day whacks you in the face. There must be respect for reality. Abide by the reliability of logical reasoning and scientific evidence, distrusting belief and being wary of opinion.

What is your bottom line? Work this out. If you are willing to be deep and meaningful, the relevant question here would be selfishness or non-selfishness? Superficially, in sport, it may be winning a medal.

Society is messed up. Politicians even acknowledge there has been a moral decline. There is no quick fix to the summer riots of 2011 that were just one symptom of many. Billions of people don't even realise that they are zombie-like. So - and here comes a small dose of reality - it will take more than one person's lifetime to bring about the kind of change that I know can be achieved. This could be at least several

hundred years ahead. Are you prepared to work really hard, with all of the associated sacrifice, for something you'll never see? If so, that's vision. And as for the 10,000 hour rule, it ultimately needs to be done by everyone. Can you be real enough to help start the long process of human advancement? Or does fantasy suddenly seem warm and cosy, offering a much easier option? Avoidance? What avoidance?

*Above and far left:*
*Even the mighty lion knows not to mess with an elephant. The reality is that size matters.*

## vi. The spirit of an adventurer

Courage and honour are also required to make the vision come true. These qualities are hard to describe. I am not meaning the adventure-for-self, perhaps involving some short-term challenge or adrenaline fix. There must be a higher goal.

Bravery is a word most often associated with fighting a battle, but it is relevant here. It is about being lion-hearted or having true grit.

Vicky would say "You need balls!" The traditional Tibetan proverb conveys the same message: "It is better to be a tiger for a day than a sheep for a thousand years." I would recommend *The Last Samurai*; although a Hollywood movie, the main characters successfully portray valour, thanks to excellent directing by Edward Zwick.

Integrity is important. In a world where bullshit and deceit is so readily accepted, there is a need for cohesion of values. Self-honesty matters. Cultivate a purity of purpose.

## vii. Hunger

A recent interviewee had finished her university studies and started work in recruitment. She had long since been haunted by the thought of having to have a career, when she really believed life should be about something bigger. She wrote to us, saying that the rat race was everything she thought it would be and worse. Her passion was wild life and she was keen to get involved. She was willing to give her all.

Our interview process worked, unfortunately or fortunately, and this young woman didn't even make it to The Oasis for a practical assessment. She was undoubtedly a good candidate to interview. We opened her eyes to the no-nonsense reality of what we do. She started to challenge the widely-accepted and narrow definition of selfishness. But the recruitment job was easy, if also unsatisfying, and she was well paid. She had moved back into the comfort of the parental home after finishing her studies. And the idea of travelling the world with friends still had appeal. She self-honestly concluded that selfishness was the dominant consideration. Her passion or hunger for helping wildlife wasn't as strong as she had wanted to believe.

If the appetite for one thing is greater than the thirst for something else, this fixes the outcome. You forget what you wrote down, etc. This is a common failing. You see it all the time in dieting. They want to be slimmer, but that chocolate cake tastes so nice. Avoidance kicks in for the millionth time. Social conditioning and the advertising of materialism is powerful and most people don't fully appreciate how little freedom of choice they actually utilise. So if you want to break free, be hungry.

*"There's still so many answers I don't know. I realise that to question is how we grow. So I step out of the ordinary."*

Proud
Heather Small

*Far left: Hunger should drive us on.*

133

*Above:* Komsberg's
animals begin with
*"a" is for aardvark...*

## viii. Be prepared

This motto was commonly associated with the Scouting and Guiding movement, due to its popularity in the twentieth century. Likewise, the UK Highways Agency uses it when warning of winter weather and also for offering best advice before undertaking a long journey. It is practical, easy to remember, and has widespread application.

Being prepared is a state of readiness to do the right thing at the right time. Often, like driving a car, this necessitates being able to employ a number of skills in combination as and when needed. This is also true when the task is to enhance psychological health. Everything that I am describing in this chapter and the next are essential qualities. They fit together, like tools in a toolbox. You can't construct a house with just a hammer, or a saw, or a screwdriver.

Those who are fluffy rely on hope. This approach is usually naive and the desired outcome is unlikely to happen or may even be rend-

ered impossible. Heart surgeons and British cycling gold medallists prefer exact knowledge and skill learned through repeated practice. Being prepared produces not only success but also a very high level of reliability.

*Above:* .....and continues through the alphabet until "z" is for zebra.

The question "What if..." is a useful prompt. It can get you thinking about preparedness. It can combat lazy mindedness and complacency. It can help push the boundaries and encourage the consideration of consequences. The chances of failure can be significantly reduced.

## ix. Never give up

Quitters never win, nor achieve anything worthwhile. Struggle is a valuable attribute, contrary to popular opinion in this "easy" world of trivial pursuits. Indeed, we have given the name Struggle to one of our Burchell's zebra at Komsberg in recognition of this key importance.

*Above: On two trips to Ngorongoro Crater in Tanzania, every early morning I went straight to the Lerai Forest. Day after day, I failed to find what I was looking for but I stayed true to my photographic vision.*
*On the final morning of my last visit, I saw two bull elephants at the base of a magnificent yellow-barked acacia tree. The crater rim can be seen in the background. This image is featured in "Wonders of Nature".*

Sally Pearson might say "It's not the bloody curse you need to worry about, it's the hurdles that can trip you up." And the minefields, of course. Jonathan Livingston Seagull crashed whilst attempting to fly faster, almost giving up his "foolish" thoughts of becoming something more worthwhile.

Paula is the co-ordinator of our animal feeders at The Oasis. When her father died, her mother urged Paula to go to work. When her dog then died, she was again counselled to go to work, rather than sit in the corner and feel sorry for herself. Her mother was at the end of her own life when Paula contacted us to get involved. Becky was about to go overseas, yet needed to provide training on how to feed our meerkats and other animals. Paula had been at her mother's bedside through the night when she passed away in the early morning. Used to facing reality and maintaining responsibility, Paula showered and changed her clothes before coming to The Oasis within a few hours of her mother's death. A year or so later, she was asked to co-ordinate the mini-team of animal feeders.

Quitting may seem to be the easier option, but the consequences will hinder and hold you back from any potential fulfillment. Giving up adds fuel to self-pity and other forms of self-centredness. Fighting through testing circumstances might appear to be more difficult, but you can learn from such trying times - including the ability to dig deep when it matters. A fighter will succeed when others have given up.

Resilience is necessary, especially as this work is long-term. Just to make clear, resilience is not the same as coping. Indeed, "cope" should be viewed as a four-letter swearword, clearly indicating that the stress of life is nearing a breakdown point. Life should rather be a process of unfolding, achieving greater involvement - not retreating. Mental toughness is a strength that grows out of the repeated practice of making correct choices. Like everything else I am outlining, it is a learned ability. There is always the freedom of choice. You can learn how to be helpless. Or, alternatively, you can learn how to be capable - and, preferably, helpful.

*Above: I was in the Lake District, getting photographic images for "Wonders of Nature". I had really bad malaria attacks for 17 years and on this particular day I was struggling. A planned walk suddenly got longer due to a foot-and-mouth disease footpath closure. Then I saw "green river". It is one of my many personal examples of "never give up".*

# 10

# More key issues

## i. Anti-hypocrisy test

*The teacher remarked to the pupil: "Your problem is that you are seeing double." "Impossible!" replied the pupil. "If that were so, there would be four suns in the sky instead of two!"*

The need for an anti-hypocrisy test should be obvious. Self-deception is just one of the various faces of avoidance. Insincerity may not be intended, but it is the inevitable outcome when some degree of ignorance remains. The problem is how to overcome this central barrier.

A reliable and complete blueprint or map is the initial requirement. Without such a guide, you'll just get lost. A practical anti-hypocrisy test is also indispensable, to be used in conjunction with the map. The best I can come up with is "actions speak louder than words". Please notice that the emphasis is on actions, plural. On-going actions will confirm success and expose failings. One (or even a few actions) is insufficient. Objective feedback is obligatory to combat delusion.

Action must follow and reflect awareness, otherwise the claimed awareness is hollow. And this action must be appropriate. If it is less than appropriate, such a cop-out will dodge the issue and thereby

*Right and far right:*
*Lions have a mighty roar. But their ability as a major predator is well proven.*

138

*Above:* A big elephant.

render the anti-hypocrisy test useless. I will be highlighting enquiry as a means of raising awareness in a forthcoming sub-section of this chapter and explaining more about appropriateness thereafter. This is page-by-page communication via a book, not some near-instant Vulcan mind-meld. So you'll obviously need to re-read this part again, if not many more times, before you understand my meaning.

Responsiveness connects awareness with action. In a world where people insist on their human rights, responsibility is often conveniently forgotten. Yet it is as important. Personal responsibility is part of being awake. There is openness or there is the closed-mindedness of avoidance. You need to open up.

What I am suggesting is much more than a series of successful heart operations or a neckful of medals. You should be thinking big, really big. Human potential is supposed to be transformative. But it rarely is this, with people instead settling for merely having an interest in the subject. Whereas real change has to be on a step-by-step basis, the framework and ultimate goal must be fully accommodated. This is a huge statement that will probably take some consideration. Over the past 30 years, I have deliberately set up a suitable structure to enable change to happen. The name of The Oasis hopefully suggests the beginning of such an intention. (And there is no opting-out. The opposite of desertification is oasification, a reclamation process of a degraded land. We opt-in, so to speak.) Those who later progress to working at Komsberg Wilderness Nature Reserve then affectionately refer to The Oasis as "the playground".

I admit there is an impasse or at least a bottleneck here. If you don't know what you're doing, you'll wander around forever and a day. Attaching yourself to a good cause is not enough. Look at what happens with humanitarian aid agencies and nature conservation organisations. The whole system is set up to accommodate selfishness. As Ericsson and colleagues have realised, you need a well-informed coach. But you also need a proper pitch to play on - not a minefield, an artist's canvas, or some virtual reality that doesn't exist. If you are serious, contact us. We are genuinely pioneering and I don't know of any other authentic attempt to suggest as an alternative. If by any chance you are reading this in the year 2414, I hope the human race is a bit smarter and a range of local "how to" centres have been set up to assist.

Before moving on, I would like to re-emphasise the crucial need for an anti-hypocrisy test in the form of "actions speak louder than words". This is perhaps indicated by the fact that these latter words WERE used as an earlier book title. I am not aware of anyone using the term "anti-hypocrisy test" before I started doing so, which must say something about the current state of spiritual or psychological awareness. I should also make clear, should any doubt remain, that such a method of self-assessment is absolutely essential at every level of change. So, for example, if you are a team member who has already been doing this work for five or ten or fifteen years, it still applies - albeit on a different, more advanced level. Avoidance is persistent and can be subtle, so the need for a reliable tool to expose it cannot be overestimated.

*"Only a life lived for others is a life worthwhile."*

Albert Einstein

## ii. Tool

Service before self is what it's all about. A common Sudanese saying is "No thanks for duty." And "A man without duty is not yet a man" sounds like it should be someone's quote (but, apparently, it isn't). What I am trying to convey is something bigger, a greater sense and application of duty. A duty to all, not just a few.

So, to make way for such a possibility, a lot of accumulated indulgences have to be dumped. Again, this can be done step-by-step. There is a false perception that sacrifice is bad and undesirable. Yet it is seen as being admirable in the case of elite athletes - although their sacrifice is made for the purpose of achieving personal glory or ambition and therefore "understandable". If you are a vegetarian, then you will have chosen to exclude all meat and fish products from your diet. This is a small but nevertheless clear example of willingly making a sacrifice for some greater good.

Letting go of limiting "me, first" attachments and preoccupations is required. On a deeper level, this is matched with a surrender towards non-selfish action. This idea of surrender is nothing new. But it has been misjudged and exploited many times in the past. So I would like to stress the need for what I might call *intelligent* surrender, which involves careful and logical thinking. A simple example of *intelligent* giving - as different from normal giving - would be when deciding to make donations to charity. Obviously, all good causes are worthwhile. But *intelligent* giving would question the appropriateness of supporting any organisation that justifies spending the money on unnecessary or high salaries, plus other dubious costs.

Surrender should not be about self-denial as such, nor annihilation of self. To repeat, non-selfishness can be thought of as one for all and all for one (even if we have to wait awhile for the "all for one" bit). Included in this concept or reality is the fact that each of us is one and therefore part of the whole. Some initial confusion is understandable because when it is said that there is a need to "die" to your former self, so to speak, this is correct - but only with regard to those limitations which prevent a fullness of being. The issue of individuality is real and not on trial here.

> "*The best way to find yourself is in the service of others.*"
>
> Mahatma Gandhi

> "*Joy can be real only if people look upon their life as a service, and have a definite object in life outside themselves and their personal happiness.*"
>
> Leo Tolstoy

Humility replaces arrogance. Sacrifice, surrender, and service before self all make good sense. Greater intelligence and consideration make it impossible to be small-minded - and you become unable to turn away from the whole. In a matter of speaking, there is a loss of freedom of choice because the question of what to do becomes blatantly obvious. The words of Neil Young's *Ohio* ring true: "How can you run when you know?" You eventually become a willing tool.

## iii.  Enquiry

The key part of what I have called "the way of *seeing* and *feeling*" is enquiry. You must question so as to expose, understand, and clarify. It is the activity of intentionally looking for answers. It is much more than curiosity. Enquiry should occur as a real question that must be answered. Your examination should be as honest and as objective as possible. And it should be urgent. As you progress, enquiry penetrates further behind the veils of illusion. This includes error-focused learning. Your mind must be active; laziness will hinder *seeing*.

Enquiry and the resulting *seeing* (and associated *feeling*) goes hand-in-hand with "actions speak louder than words" as an anti-hypocrisy test. The two are interrelated as key mechanisms for changing. *Seeing* should trigger *feeling* and greater action, this then prompting further enquiry. And so on. Each aspect should be mutually developed and fine-tuned to higher and higher levels.

Uncovering the limitations of selfishness is easier said than done. The justification of avoidance will get in the way, keeping you blind or partially sighted. The trouble with most people is that they will not listen to what the trouble with them is. And I am urging you to undermine your own defensiveness, to go against the emotional reaction of keeping things safe. Become constructively dissatisfied.

I have written more about *seeing* and *feeling* in my first two books, which can be referred to for further explanation. If you have an initial difficulty in understanding what I mean by *seeing*, keep re-reading and trying to grasp how it works. Once mastered, the effects are liberating and powerful.

> *"We make a living by what we get, but we make a life by what we give."*
>
> Winston Churchill

143

## iv.  Picture building

After enquiry, what do you do with the answers? The resulting bits of awareness or understanding need to be linked together, piece by piece like a jigsaw puzzle. Gradually, they start to form a detailed picture or map of what is going on - and not going on. Keep the process going and be wary of settling for a certain level of comprehension. Push to complete building the picture.

The ability to link is the standout point here. Everyone knows the wise saying "You can lead a horse to water but you can't make it drink." I slightly adapt it to "You can lead a horse to water but you can't make it think." And then I move it a step further on with "You can lead a horse to water but you can't make it link." Avoidance, of course, is the usual suspect. Linking is part of a solution for the great escape from prison and the barbed wire fencing that surrounds it. The jigsaw pieces act like wooden slats from beds used to shore up the walls of the escape tunnel, without which there would be collapse and continued imprisonment.

Linking focuses extra attention on individual realisations that might otherwise slip away. It reinforces awareness. Implications and conseq- uences are revealed. Patterns and mechanisms become obvious. The linking together of bits of understanding enables both a wide and a specific in-depth view of issues that could easily be missed or glossed over. With sufficient practice, the effects of avoidance are weakened. A new "Why couldn't I see this before?" perspective dawns - and then grows stronger.

## v.  Appropriateness and preferences

We were working in the Himalayas of Nepal. Coincidentally, I spent three evenings in the company of a group of top Japanese businessmen in their early sixties who were on a brief vacation. On the final evening, I asked each of them for their best advice for life. Although all were very successful, one man had stood out to me above the others and I still remember his contribution: "Burn yourself to ashes."

*"Tear down your own little walls that keep you from being a part of it all."*

*Close To It All*
Melanie

**Far right:**
*Illumination can make a lot of difference.*

*Above: It is appropriate to provide wild animals with a lot of space for them to flourish. This family of elephants was photographed at Amboseli, with the famous Kilimanjaro in the background.*

Over the centuries, there have been various moral guidelines based on cultural, religious, political, or philosophical doctrines. These have often been rigid, involving "Thou shall not" commandments. As intelligence and awareness grows, we look for a less dogmatic approach. Once an individual has sufficiently matured to be able to understand the complexities of life, including the limitations of selfish psychology and the better option of non-selfishness, ethical or moral development can then proceed with the help of two pointers: appropriateness and preferences.

Appropriateness must come first, in keeping with what you know of the bigger picture. We're back to "service before self" here - or, to put it even more clearly, need before want. This provides the means of sorting out different priorities. When there is unblinkered awareness, the course of action is usually obvious. The added benefit of experience may help, but the general direction is blatantly clear. On a much deeper level than the popular slogan, you just do it. The most appropriate needs come first and so on. And don't forget what I've said about the subject of *intelligent* surrender and giving, just to remind you about linking everything together in a coherent framework.

Preference comes second. This can be applied to deciding between two different but equally appropriate options, although it more usually refers to personal appetite or taste. There should be opportunity for individual interests or inclinations. Preference offers an advanced version of "I want" or desire. As appropriateness comes first, compulsive tendencies are extinguished without losing any zest for life.

Two superficial examples of my own will hopefully illustrate what I mean. The first takes us back to 1985 after I had returned to the UK from my first trip to famine-stricken Ethiopia. I was working flat out, at least 18 hours a day or more. A lot needed doing and I was burning myself to ashes. But - mainly to make a point to those who were close to me - I took off one hour each week for myself. I watched *Dallas*, never having done so before. I don't remember why, but I do recall it was after the "Who shot JR?" saga; JR and Bobby Ewing were embroiled in a winner-takes-all battle for the family oil business. My fundraising talks would be scheduled for a particular day and time, sometimes clashing with the weekly episode of this television series. When this happened, a friend would video tape it for me and my hour would be spent watching it at some time during the seven days. One for all and all for one is a constant reality for me - and I'm a little part of it and do exist.

My second example is that I drink Coca Cola. Out of a can and with ice. If I'm offered it from a plastic bottle, I'd prefer water, because it tastes different. At least to me. And no disrespect to the competition, but Pepsi just isn't the same. As for Virgin Cola, forget it. I wasn't impressed, Richard, although I still listen to *Tubular Bells*. Becky and I frequently consume "no name" supermarket products to save money, but you wouldn't catch me drinking Asda cola or anything similar. We wait until a half price offer becomes available, then bulk buy and store. I never forget the 15-year-old Ethiopian girl who died in my arms and if our charity work ever hit rock bottom, I'd stop drinking Coke in an instant and switch to water - diverting what little money I spend on myself to whatever would be appropriate.

> *"It's better to burn out than to fade away."*
>
> *My My, Hey Hey*
> Neil Young

## vi.  Perspective and approach

Once you've grasped enough of these key issues, here's a simple way of proceeding. There are two basic psychological strategies: selfishness and non-selfishness. So your perspective on life is either one or the other: selfish or non-selfish. Easy. And there are two basic attitudes to life: "I can" and "I can't". So your approach is either one or the other: "I can" or "I can't". Again, easy.

It gets slightly more complicated at this point. Combine the two, use your brain to the best of your ability, and the sensible perspective and approach will be non-selfishness and "I can". Still quite easy, eh?! Anything less than this boils down to a cowardly excuse or apology. "Be just and fear not."

I came up with "perspective and approach" for a pre-Christmas meeting with my colleagues some time ago. Another year, I thought up the "torch on, torch off" story. We all know that a torch is needed to see what is going on and to find your way in the dark. But a torch is only a torch in practical terms if it has enough power. A torch with no batteries isn't really a torch at all. It must have sufficient power so that the beam of light illuminates the way ahead. If this isn't the case and you're walking around the homestead at Komsberg after dark, for example, you possibly risk standing on a snake that you couldn't see. The batteries don't have to be fully charged all of the time, but if they drop below an acceptable level then you no longer possess a functioning torch.

Going back to the "I can" bit of perspective and approach, I remember the Wing Commander in charge of the Royal Air Force mission in Ethiopia when I was first there in January 1985. His attitude was excellent and he helped a lot. Indeed, the overall RAF effort made me feel proud to be British. The Russians had 30 transport planes based at Addis Ababa. The British had two C-130 Hercules aircraft by comparison, yet were doing more. When a bird of prey smashed a gaping hole in the nose of a Hercules that I was travelling in one day - I was actually in the cockpit at the time - it was all patched up by the engineers, ready to fly by dawn the next day. Anyway, back to the Wing Commander. His motto was "The answer's 'yes', just ask the question."

*"Perhaps a better world*
*is drawing near.*
*Just as easily*
*it could all disappear,*
*Along with*
*whatever meaning*
*you might have found.*
*Don't let*
*the uncertainty*
*turn you around."*

*For A Dancer*
Jackson Browne

## vii.  Scale

*Above:* The tiny
malachite kingfisher is
one of my favourite birds.

A common fallacy is underestimating the scale of what this involves.
I am sensitive to this point and do whatever I can to prevent such
misconception. But it still happens, time after time. Jonathan has seen
it occur in many workshops, regardless of how well someone responds
to what I've been saying or how intelligent they might be. Deanne was
a co-director of our work for many years, living with a rare incurable
cancer for most of the time. She urged me, when we talked the other
day, to accentuate that many people arrogantly think they understand
when they have actually only scratched the surface. She stressed that
most people read my books in the same manner, missing layer after
layer of depth or meaning. Indeed, Deanne admitted to me not long
ago that it took her about two years before she really knew what I
was bleating on about. And she had had many glimpses or partial
experiences of oneness herself, earlier in her life; she was 48 years of
age when she got involved.

> *"You must be the change you wish to see in the world."*
>
> Mahatma Gandhi

Psychologists and other experts are starting to get the idea. But the one thing that is frequently ignored or trivialised is the need for deeper meaning and purpose. Yet this is the mother of all keys. Perhaps they are scared to risk professional and personal credibility by talking about the concept of one for all and all for one. It's just too far off or perhaps unrealistic in this selfish world of billions. More likely, it is raw avoidance that gets in the way and their thinking doesn't get that far. British cyclists can do it for the team, as well as for personal glory, but the word "team" doesn't somehow extend to everyone and the whole of life. So, they're on the detective trail of finding clues - but haven't yet realised that the crime of the century is being committed.

Becky knows well that if people have any kind of opt-out clause they will use it to minimise their relationship with life. Eminem got it spot on when he rapped "Success is my only motherfucking option, failure's not." And I think his expletive is helpful.

Don't confuse awareness with achievement. The anti-hypocrisy test of actions speak louder than words will combat this error, if it is taken far enough and repeatedly applied as intended. Consideration should be given to a line in the proverbial sand; above is acceptable and below is not. The importance of self-respect and the need for a deeper approach to self-image should likewise be addressed.

Scale exists. Human potential is real. The inherent benefits for us all are massive. How you choose to apply your mind is, quite rightly, up to you. What you do and don't do will seriously impact on others through consequences, whether you realise this or not. Think big.

**Far right:** *Deanne at the base of the incredible General Sherman Tree in California's Sequoia National Park. This is the largest living thing on planet Earth. Again, can you "think big"?*

150

# Conclusion

What is it like being enlightened? My usual response when I have been asked this question has been to re-direct attention back to the questioner, suggesting that the matter of "how to" is more important. Occasionally, I've given the short reply of "normal" - which, for me, is true. But what's normal?

I initially studied biology, ecology, and psychology at university, eventually changing courses. I recently tried to track down the woman who was in charge of us for psychology. The two former heads of the department were helpful and somewhat intrigued by my interest after all these years. We spent a few days emailing each other, recalling and questioning memories from the past, eventually narrowing down the identity of the woman. Unfortunately, I was informed that she had moved from the field of psychology into law shortly after I knew her and there the trail went cold. On a couple of occasions, back in the mid 1970s, she pronounced my coursework essays as "unmarkable". I had apparently gone way beyond what was being taught into unknown territory. When I later decided to change courses, she tried to talk me out of it - saying that, if I continued my training, I could significantly contribute to psychology. I never mentioned anything about what was happening to me at the time, but she had obviously figured out that something was odd.

*Right and far right:*
*Happy, the orphaned baby black-backed jackal, and with Becky at his first visit to a waterhole.*

When we started work in South Africa in 1992 with the geometric tortoise, I wrote a letter to the owner of a private farm and nature reserve asking if they would kindly accommodate us. The wealthy owner passed it to his manager for comment. We stayed there and it became the regular base for our annual field trips until we established The Tortoise Farm years later. At the end of our second visit, Mike (the manager) produced my original letter and showed us his comment pencilled on the reverse side as feedback to his boss's request for his opinion. "Probably just another couple of conservationists wanting a free holiday" was his best guess. He already knew many conservationists and it was a reasonable response. When we first arrived, Mike admitted to being taken aback as he saw we were always on the go. And our early results were real and impressive. He told us that his sceptical curiosity was aroused on our return, but again saw we were working non-stop. Showing us his potentially embarrassing remark on the back of the letter, Mike said "I've come to the conclusion that you're simply here to help save the geometric tortoise."

*Above: I took this image of the geometric tortoise eating on my first ever field trip to South Africa.*

*Far left. Sundews are just one of numerous flower species that we are also protecting at The Tortoise Farm.*

*Above:* Rapid growth of the human population means more food is needed. Natural habitat in Kenya has been replaced with wheatfields like this one. How long will these flat-topped acacias remain before also disappearing?

So I could say that I'm simple, which would be true in many ways. Alternatively, I once said to Vicky "I just don't avoid." This would be a better answer. My own preference, however, would be four words from a song by Jackson Browne: "Waiting here for everyman."

But this has never been about me, as I wrote in the introduction to this book - although I have tried to say something about the "adventures of a hero", as promised, and not too much about the "how to" stuff. However, before switching it obviously back to you for a few final words of guidance, I will say one more thing about what it's like being non-selfish. Sarah used to suggest I add this as a token offering. The personal benefits are also huge, although I must insist that this isn't the main point. In over 33 years of being like this, I haven't met anyone else that is anywhere near as "happy" or "big" as myself.

Being a pioneering oddity is not ideal. Non-selfishness will best flourish when the stupidity and back-stabbing of "me, first" is finished and the human race has collectively evolved to become *Homo liberalis* or whatever the name will be. Meanwhile, you are a stranger in a

strange land. You will be misunderstood. But at least you understand. One down, 7 billion to go, is a start. A way forward exists. There is light at the end of the tunnel, no matter how far off. Always look on the bright side, etc.

Other would-be pioneers, as I have already explained, need to learn to stand up and be counted. Trailblazing is never easy. It isn't always comfortable being an outcast. But pioneers have to come from somewhere. Role models are essential. Someone has to do it. A number of "someone's", in fact. Progress is always preferable to stagnation. And, meanwhile, today's "normal" consciousness stinks.

You already know that we have named one of our Burchell's zebra Struggle. We've called another of these delightful and intelligent wild animals Avoidance Doesn't Work to stress the point. I was fortunate to be at Komsberg when he was born and therefore able to photograph him soon afterwards. If I used four words to best describe what it's like being me - waiting here for everyman - my best advice to you can be summed up in just three. Avoidance doesn't work.

*Above:* *Just born.*
*Avoidance Doesn't Work.*

# Acknowledgements

Many thanks to all of my colleagues for their usual support. Three deserve special mention. Becky, as always, gives everything. Jonathan reliably produced whatever was asked of him. Vicky's enthusiasm added bits here and there.

Patrick Mohony yet again kindly and patiently guided me through all of my software questions regarding layout and design.

I would recommend listening to all of the songs that have been mentioned throughout the book. Music can help inspire, if nothing else.

Please see *Holding On* and *Wonders of Nature* if anyone is interested in my photographic notes. My best advice to any aspiring photographer, however, is to develop the abilities outlined in the "key issues" chapters.

*Above:*
*I have fortunately seen and photographed the amazing but sadly endangered African wild dog on several occasions.*

*Far left:*
*Elephant scratching, Ngorongoro Crater.*

*Overleaf:*
*Cheetah and cubs.*

# Further reading and websites

*Human Potential - the search for that "something more"* £6.99
*Actions Speak Louder Than Words* £6.99
*What Will It Take? A Deeper Approach To Nature Conservation* £6.99
*Wonders of Nature* £25.00
*Holding On* £25.00

Proceeds from the sale of the above books, as well as this one,
including the author's/photographer's royalties,
will be used for our charitable work.
We purposely work non-paid.

www.wildlifeforall.org
www.thehumanpotentialtrust.org
www.visitkomsberg.org
www.lettuceleaf.org

Email: wildlifeforall@hotmail.com